MODERN LOVE

Danielle Vieira

MODERN LOVE

our avoidant world

Translation: Lucas Machado
Review: Joyce Epifanio Rodrigues de Almeida
English cover: Luiza Amaral
Graphic design: Vinicius Torquato
Interior images: Danielle Vieira

Vieira, Danielle
Modern Love: Our Avoidant World / Danielle Vieira.
São Paulo, 2026.
192 p.

ISBN 978-65-02-13501-3

1. Love, social aspects 2. Psychoanalysis 3. Attachment
4. Psychology I. Title

26-365614.0 CDD-158.1

Systematic catalog index:
1. Love, social aspects

contato@daniellevieira.com.br | www.daniellevieira.com.br

To Marcos, who taught me, in practice, what secure love is;
To Rapha, the creative spark behind this book.
And to all those who continue searching for a possible love.

To all the people who entrusted me with their love stories over these years. Especially those I met while living as a nomad, from Brazil to Australia, from Tunisia to Germany.

I am grateful for every encounter, every conversation, and every connection that became engines of creation and sources of inspiration. I hope you find, in this book, a fragment of yourselves, recognized and cared for.

Table of Contents

"The colibri kisses the flower so it does not collide."

– Pedro Gabriel, Brazilian poet, *My Name Is Antonio.*

Introduction

Hummingbird love and modernity

This book is born out of love that could not flourish, not due to the lack of affection, but due to the impossibility of sustaining it. Born from the experience of giving yourself entirely to love in a world that avoids being whole. Just like the hummingbird, who performs a spectacle of seduction with acrobatic flights, vibrating his wings at unique frequencies and impressing the females with his dance, but vanishing after mating. Modern love is intense, quick, dazzling and ephemeral.

I write this book because what I call here "modern love" has become a game of who cares less. We have created a problematic culture of emotional detachment as self-protection, which has become a strategy of seduction under the market logic of consuming people, social media, and dating apps. And, for these and other reasons, relationships, and people, are becoming increasingly disposable.

We have never talked so much about freedom, and we have never been so imprisoned by our own fears. We have never been so lonely and longing for love. At the same time, we have never been so afraid of "being with", of depending on another person.

To love and to be loved seem increasingly unlikely, although it is also one of our most vital needs. We have been captured by the idea of romantic love, a love that does not require too much work, that is easygoing, low maintenance, that only satisfies, but should not demand too much from us. Love has been reduced to the logic of dopamine, of seduction, of the illusion of possibilities, of excess, of addiction to attention: short messages, hurried encounters, fleeting emotions and lasting silences. Showing affection has become "too much vulnerability", while being detached is trendy.

This work is based on personal stories, both mine and my friends'. It is also based on my psychoanalytic listening to so many patients throughout these years of clinical practice, witnessing, up close, so many heartbreaks, mismatches, disillusionments and exhaustion, and on the exhaustion that has become increasingly evident. An exhaustion that comes from believing in and betting on possible love, a love without games, a love that stays.

I write for you who loved truly, who gave yourself fully, without fear, or even with fear, but found walls where you had hoped to build bridges. I write for you who loved someone who did not know what to do with the love they were receiving and ran away. And I also write for those who still do not know how to receive love, how to stay, but who feel a deep desire for genuine connection and live in an endless search for affection.

I write for the human being who, in their natural state, craves strong, secure bonds that create a sense of belonging.

Perhaps you have been taken over by the confusion of having lived something so intense and true and then being left adrift, without understanding the ending, without knowing where the affection that was there went. Without knowing whether you misunderstood it, or whether the other person failed to act and communicate with you properly.

This book is for you who have already been ghosted, or suffered *love bombing* followed by *ghosting*. For you who have been in a situationship that felt more like a real relationship, but in the end heard, "I don't want a serious relationship." I write to you who are somebody's *premium hookup* or have one or more *premium hookups*, without really committing.

I write for you who have accepted crumbs from someone (the famous breadcrumbing), or who have kept someone like that only out of neediness. I write for you who like someone who does not reply to your messages, but views and/or likes your stories on social media. I write for you who collect people instead of truly connecting, or who have already been part of someone else's collection. I write for all of us who are immersed in romantic illusions and disillusionments.

I write for you who pretend to be nonchalant only to win someone over, when in reality you feel more than you can admit. I write for you who want to understand all these new terms that describe situations that, at times, border on the absurd, something between comic and tragic.

Together, we will dive into the epidemic of a world that avoids affection, avoids frustration, fears vulnerability, and moves further and further away from a possible love. After all, what is a possible love? Through attachment theory, neuroscience and a dash of philosophy and poetry, we will discover, together, how we, as a society and as individuals, got here, where we are heading and how we can change this modern love scenario – maybe starting with ourselves.

This is not a technical book; it's a crossing, a gentle stroke for those who have lived through one (or many) *almosts*. A small map for those who need to cross the turbulent ocean of emotions and affections and (re)discover the path back to their own heart.

(IN)EVITABLE

Chapter 1

The society of the almost

"Everyone has an almost love.
A story that, by a whim of fate or
by our own negligence, did not happen
But that's not the problem. The problem
is what it does to us.
How can a story that never really happened
keep other stories from happening?
How can a love that went wrong make us think
that no other love will ever work?
When we are children, we are afraid of ghosts,
of spirits of people who have already died.
But when we grow up, we realize that
the ghosts are different. Ghosts of people
who died inside us, but still visit us.
And what scares us the most is not their presence.
What scares us the most is the absence this presence makes"
– **Marcos Bulhões, Brazilian poet and chronicler.**

My great friend Bruna once told me: "Girl, what really hurts is the *almost*-something"; almost boyfriends, almost together, almost love. As Sarah Westphal (2002), author of the chronicle *Almost* says: "Even worse than the conviction of the no, or the uncertainty of the maybe, is the delusion of the almost; it is the almost that bothers me, that saddens me, that kills me by bringing up everything that could have been and wasn't."[1]

1 The text was originally published in Portuguese on Sarah Westphal's blog in 2002, but it can be found at this link: https://tinyurl.com/5n85znvv.

The almost inhabits this space between encounter and loss, between promises and emptiness, between idealization and disillusionment. The almost is a lukewarm place that, in modern love, has been mistaken for a safe place, where we offer love only to the extent that we can control it (or think we can control it). In the modern logic of turning everything into capital, love has become a high-risk financial investment: one must evaluate the return, measure the investment, analyze the market and, preferably, not invest all capital in a single place. The subject is driven to administer himself as a company, invest more in himself, manage his emotions as resources and avoid losses at any cost. The maxim of "I am master of myself" contrasts with the human condition itself and with the unconscious logic that we have desires, feelings and thoughts that we simply do not control, as Freud reminds us: "the ego is not master in its own house."[2] We may even choose what we do with what we feel, in theory, but we do not control how we feel in relation to the other. Still, there is a premise, which is applied in modern love, that seems to have as its main objective protecting our "affective capital":

- *You can't get attached.*
- *You can't show your feelings.*
- *You must not want.*
- *You can't answer quickly.*
- *You must not commit.*

2 Freud, 1917.

All of this crosses the imaginary line of emotional control and clears the path for yet another *almost*, with justifications to avoid affection:

- *It was too intense.*
- *I don't want commitment.*
- *I don't want to lose my freedom.*
- *I don't need a relationship.*
- *I thought we could keep this casual.*

In short: if it is real affection, it cannot continue.

Everyone wants to be loved, but it seems that few want or are able to be vulnerable enough to love. Everyone wants the right person (as if someone could simply show up ready-made), but few are willing to do the work, in themselves and, together with the other, build something of value, instead of continuing in an incessant search for the ideal match.

Everything is ephemeral, everything is *stories*, but the *almost* is not a lukewarm place, as it seems. The *almost* hurts and, quite often, traumatizes more than when a cycle is completed. And I use the word trauma here as a rupture, that can be big or small.

When a relationship ends prematurely, it is usually for small reasons or even "for no reason at all"; because of this, affection is interrupted, our expectations break, and we give space to the projection of what could have been. It is as if we were listening to that song from the 2000s, the one that hits deep in the chest and, when it reaches its peak, the chorus, the moment when you are about to sing and let everything out, someone goes there and turns off the sound. We are outraged! Who turned it off? Why did they turn it off? But I love this song, the song was good, we were enjoying it. How? Why? The questions remain in the air and, quite often, we find no answers.

The almost-somethings occupy a place in our fantasy; we project what could have been and fill the unexplained emptiness with idealizations (usually with scenarios of a perfect life). When there is no closure, we cannot work through the grief. We leave everything open. And our brain does not like unfinished business: we keep revisiting the messages and the memory of the moments we lived, searching for a solution or an understanding of why it went wrong.

The almost leaves a somewhat cruel thread of hope, one that activates in us the cycle of expectation for an intermittent affection, the need to be chosen in order to reverse the rejection we experienced.

Then, after many *almosts*, we learn to protect ourselves, not to feel so much, to pretend that we don't have any expectations, that we don't care. We adopt a nonchalant attitude, a word that comes from the French *nonchaloir*. Nonchalant means, literally, "to not care", "to not be shaken"; a certain elegant indifference. We fight at all costs to sustain the image that we are immune to the other, as a certain kind of affective power.

A quick search on the internet is enough to find videos teaching how to be nonchalant in order to attract partners, in a behavior of rejecting the other that seems to have become attractive and widely spread. So far, nothing new. It is a fact that, in romances across generations, there is always one who rejects and another who feels compelled to conquer. A certain mystery is part of the game of seduction, an unpredictable dynamic that allows the erotic dance of love and conquest to take place. The problem begins when this behavior becomes established in the dynamic as a form of affective power; when, after moving beyond the flirting stage, we continue using the *modus operandi* of avoiding the other and pretending we do not care. All of this so that we may be desired or, very often unconsciously, so that we do not go deeper into a relationship, do not get involved, do not commit—not only to the other, but above all to ourselves.

If there is one thing a relationship brings us, it is the challenge of facing our own limitations, where we are flawed, insufficient, our insecurities, our fears, and everything we spend our entire lives trying to avoid knowing about ourselves. A relationship works like a mirror: it exposes us to the best and the worst of ourselves and has the power to disarm even our oldest defenses, because when we truly desire the other, we become vulnerable: to loss, to rejection, to uncertainty and, above all, to lack.

We are a whole generation trying to love with protection, trying to kiss while wearing a helmet, to hug while wearing armor; we protect ourselves so much that we avoid love before it can even happen. "It was almost love, it was almost love," as that Rag'n'Bone Man song says. But why do we prefer to remain in the almost? Is it really a choice, or a new symptom of a society that does not know how to stay? What do we avoid when we remain at the border? What is missing for us to go beyond? What do we lose?

The almost also expands into other areas of modern life, when we choose a job that does not fulfill us, does not challenge us, but offers a certain stability that keeps us from taking risks and going beyond. Almost graduated, almost a doctor, almost a lawyer, almost... But we give up before the end, we change so many times that we become lost amid so many possibilities. We move on to the next thing without finishing the first, without working through the grief, without closing anything; the next course, the next book, the next match, the next job, the next trip, the next thing that promises to relieve our emptiness and fill something that is missing.

POSSIBLE LOVE

If we truly want to sustain a relationship and stay with someone, we will necessarily need to change, adjust, evolve and work on ourselves in order to build something. Being in a relationship takes work, and loving is, to some extent, "knowing what one does not want to know".

Resilience, or the lack of it, is an important trait that helps us understand, at least a little, so many almosts. The word comes from the Latin *resilire*, formed by re, meaning again or backward, and *salire,* meaning to leap or jump. Literally, it means "to jump back, to retreat, to return to the previous state"; a certain elasticity that physics describes very well: certain bodies, when subjected to pressure or deformation, recover their original shape once the force is removed. Psychology appropriated this term to describe a capacity that is essential for crossing the difficulties of life: to overcome, to adapt, to be flexible in the face of conflict; the famous "it bends, but does not break." But this capacity seems to have been diminishing over time. In general, we have been managing lack and frustration poorly, because in the modern world there is no lack, or at least that is the discourse we have been sold. There is a product for everything, a solution for every problem. We create the illusion that something or someone will complete us and, when we discover that it is not quite like that, we replace it, searching for the next promise of completeness. And yet, many times, we decide not to take risks. We want to ride a bicycle around the world, but on a bicycle with training wheels, so we do not fall or get hurt. And if we have to climb a mountain, it is better not to go at all.

The formula of modern life seems to be to avoid risk at all costs and stay wherever things are easier; but no one has yet invented insurance for loving. For this reason, love seems increasingly risky, and we gradually lose not only the ability to take risks and to love, but also forget what it is like to be loved; because the capacity to receive love is also an essential and overlooked ability, one that needs to be developed.

We are so used to being excited all the time, with our nervous system activated for danger, for novelty, for the roller coaster of emotions, that we seem to be unlearning how to relax in a secure bond.

In the society of the almost, we live through an avoidant epidemic of affection; stories become confusion on one side and silence on the other. And the deeper connection remains only through a viewed story. Relationships become a threat to our individuality, rather than an opportunity for growth and discovery. What seems to be merely a social phenomenon actually has deeper psychological roots. The way we relate today is not only a product of haste and the logic of consumption.

It also translates a pattern of how we learned, from very early on, to deal with affection, with presence and absence, and the way we respond, in different ways, to love, care, conflict, rejection and abandonment. In the next chapter, we will explore more deeply how almost-love is directly connected to the avoidant epidemic.

Chapter 2

The avoidant epidemic

"I consider the desire to be loved and cared for as an integral part of human nature throughout adult life."
– **John Bowlby, British psychiatrist and psychoanalyst.**

The word "avoid" comes from the Latin verb *evitare*, which means "to evade", "to escape" or "to dodge." The Latin verb *evitare* is a combination of ex ("out") and *vitare* ("avoid"), indicating the act of fleeing from or moving away from something or someone.

To understand this epidemic symptom of our time, we need to dive a little deeper into the attachment types—also called attachment styles—which refer to the ways we interpret and position ourselves within our relationship to the other. The foundations of attachment theory can help us understand how we bond with others and how we react in different situations within a romantic relationship.

Attachment theory was developed by John Bowlby, British psychologist and psychiatrist, in the 1950s.[3] He began researching the impact that primary bonds have on our emotional and relational life. In practical terms, Bowlby postulated that the form through which we establish bonds with our caregivers in the first months and years of life will serve as a mold, an internal model,

3 Bowlby, 1982.

that will shape the way we seek, interpret, build and keep relationships throughout our lives.

Bowlby worked in a psychiatric hospital in the first years of his career, and it was there that he found inspiration for his innovative work on attachment, by observing that two children under his care presented different and striking behaviors: while one was emotionally distant and had little emotional expression, the other one was constantly around him, to the point of being nicknamed by his colleagues "Bowlby's shadow".

The work of the British psychiatrist was strongly influenced by Konrad Lorenz, an Austrian zoologist and ethologist who showed that attachment is instinctive. He developed the concept of *imprinting*: through his observation of birds, especially of greylag geese. He discovered that goslings formed an immediate and seemingly irreversible bond with the first moving object they saw after hatching, usually the mother, though it could also be the researcher himself or a substitute object. This showed that early attachment is an innate behavior, biologically programmed to ensure the offspring's survival.

In Lorenz's research, Bowlby saw clear evidence that human attachment would also have an instinctive, evolutionary, and biological basis, not just a psychological one. This reinforced his idea that human babies have an innate attachment system, activated to guarantee proximity to the caregiver as a strategy of protection and survival. A newborn does not need the mother only for feeding; the newborn also desires the caregiver-child connection that forms between them. Thus, Bowlby, together with psychologist Mary Ainsworth, sought to understand what happened to children when this essential need was not met.

This concept was further developed by the work of Harry Harlow, an American psychologist whose experiments carried out between the 1950s and 1960s brought striking evidence about the nature of attachment.

Harlow wanted to understand what really creates the bond between mothers and children: was it only the satisfaction of physical needs such as feeding, or was there something deeper, such as emotional comfort? To answer this question, he created a controlled environment with newborn monkeys separated from their biological mothers, immediately after birth. This laboratory gave rise to what became known as the "surrogate mother experiment."

The "Surrogate Mother Experiment"

Harlow developed two artificial "surrogate mothers" for the monkeys, which were put in the same cage:

- The "Wire Mother", made with rigid wire and equipped with a baby bottle that provided milk.
- The "Cloth Mother", covered with soft cloth, that simulated a welcoming touch, but did not provide food.

Although both of them were available for the monkeys all the time, results revealed a strong preference for the "cloth mother."

- **Comfort vs. Feeding:** the monkeys spent most of the time clinging to the "cloth mother", seeking emotional comfort. They approached the "wire mother" only to feed quickly, returning immediately afterward to the "cloth mother."
- **Stress response:** when faced with stressful situations, such as loud sounds or unfamiliar environments, the monkeys ran to the "cloth mother" in search of safety. This contact significantly reduced signs of stress.
- **Emotional development:** monkeys deprived of emotional comfort presented abnormal behavior, such as difficulty with social interactions, anxiety and aggressiveness. Those who were able to interact with the "cloth mother," however, showed greater emotional balance.

In addition to comfort, the "cloth mother" provided a sense of safety, a concept Bowlby called a "secure base." From an evolutionary perspective, cultivating and maintaining strong relationships brings advantages for both survival and reproduction. For this reason, Bowlby's work focused on the human desire to seek contact, love, support, and comfort in others—the innate human need for connection and belonging and one of the main driving forces of individual behavior. The way this initial bond is experienced can generate different attachment styles, which we will briefly explore below.

Attachment types or styles

It is important to emphasize that each of the four attachment styles has typical traits and characteristics. However, a person does not always fit 100% into a single category; attachment is a spectrum, and it is possible to move between styles or express them with different degrees of intensity.

- **Secure attachment** – develops when the caregiver is consistent, responsive, and attuned to the baby's needs. The child learns that the world is a reliable place and that seeking support from others is not dangerous. In adulthood, those who experienced secure attachment tend to feel comfortable developing intimacy and mutual dependence, balancing autonomy and connection.
- **Anxious attachment (or ambivalent/preoccupied)** – develops when the caregiver is inconsistent; sometimes present and sensitive, at other times indifferent or unpredictable. The baby grows up unsure of when and how they will be met and begins to make every effort to maintain proximity to the other. In adult life, this translates into fear of abandonment, an intense search for reassurance, and difficulty trusting the stability of bonds.
- **Avoidant attachment (or dismissive/disconnected)** – occurs when the caregiver often ignores or rejects the child's emotional needs. To protect themselves from the pain of

rejection, the baby learns to suppress requests for help and connection. In adulthood, they tend to value independence excessively, avoiding emotional closeness and distrusting the need for intimate bonds.

- **Disorganized attachment (or fearful-avoidant)** – appears when the caregiver is, at the same time, a source of comfort and of fear, as in situations of abuse or trauma. The child becomes confused, without a coherent strategy for dealing with the bond. In adult life, this usually generates relationships marked by ambivalence, in which the desire for closeness coexists with an intense fear of intimacy and pain.

Understanding the many faces of bonds helps us understand how each attachment style formed in childhood will manifest in adult life and in relationships, especially in romantic relationships.

Manifestations of Attachment in Adult Life

Attachment behavior in childhood is expressed in adult life and becomes more visible when the adult faces situations involving fear, change, or conflict, as in cases of loss, for example. These extreme and challenging situations are processed better when there is, or once has been, emotional support and trust in family members, friends, or partners.

Anxious/preoccupied

Adults with an anxious attachment style tend to have a negative view of themselves and a positive view of others. This means they may see their partner as their "better half." Because they believe they are less worthy of love than others, the idea of living without the partner (or of being alone in general) generates high levels of anxiety. In other words, they have a deep fear of abandonment. To mitigate this fear, people with anxious attachment seek intense security in their relationships. The partner's attention, care and responsiveness work as a "remedy" for their anxiety. On the other hand, perceiving a lack of support or intimacy leads them to excessive attachment behaviors, emotional neediness and a constant search for reaffirmation of being loved.

In short, they deeply value bonds, but they are often hypervigilant about threats to emotional security, living preoccupied with the possibility that they will not be loved back with the same intensity.

Avoidant/dismissive

People with an avoidant or dismissive attachment style tend to have a positive view of themselves, but a negative view of others. Thus, they cultivate a strong feeling of independence and self-sufficiency, especially on the emotional level.

Those with avoidant attachment believe they do not need a relationship to feel complete; they do not want to depend on others, nor do they want others to depend on them, avoiding the search for support, recognition, or emotional shelter in social relationships.

In adult life, they often avoid intimacy or emotional closeness and may withdraw from a relationship when they perceive that the other person is developing some kind of emotional dependence. They also tend to suppress or hide their emotions in situations potentially charged with affection or conflict.

Disorganized/fearful-avoidant

People with disorganized attachment alternate between the traits of anxious and avoidant styles, according to their mood and to circumstances. Thus, they manifest confusing and ambiguous behaviors in their interpersonal bonds.

For these adults, the partner and the relationship itself are simultaneous sources of desire and fear. On one hand, they want closeness and intimacy; on the other, they have difficulty trusting and relying on others. They frequently struggle to identify and regulate their emotions and tend to avoid deep emotional bonds because of an intense fear of getting hurt.

Secure

The previous three styles – anxious, avoidant and disorganized – are considered insecure, since they make it difficult to create and maintain healthy bonds. Secure attachment, in contrast, implies being comfortable with expressing oneself emotionally. Adults with this style can trust their partners and allow their partners to trust them. Relationships with people who have secure attachment are usually characterized by honesty, tolerance and emotional closeness. Even though they value bonds, they don't fear loneliness. They have a positive view of themselves and of others, do not seek constant validation, and are able to identify and regulate their emotions, often helping the other person do the same.

Flexibility also needs to be included in the evaluation of attachment styles. The theory also recognizes that change is possible. Life experiences throughout adolescence and adulthood can help modify and strengthen attachment styles, even when an insecure style was established in childhood. We also need to understand that, as maturity comes, we become more secure and more self-confident, and the way we experience attachment can migrate from one type to another. In short, we should not see this map of attachment as something rigid.

With this cartography of human connection in mind, some questions inevitably arise:

Why, instead of moving toward secure attachment, do we seem to be oscillating more and more between the anxious and avoidant poles? Why do so many people live relationships marked by emotional storms on one side and emotional withdrawal on the other?

Maybe the answer lies in several explanations, among them, a childhood marked by inconsistent care. For many of us, the first emotional bonds were characterized by emotionally unavailable caregivers: parents who were absent, fragile, distracted, overwhelmed by work or practical life issues, or even physically present, but unable to provide consistent emotional nurturing; parents who were not able to regulate their own emotions and, therefore, were unable to transmit this ability to their children.

In a culture that, for decades, treated affection as weakness, many children grew up learning that expressing emotions was not safe (the typical "Stop crying, or I'll give you something to cry about") or that relying on others could be dangerous, suffocating, uncertain and doomed to failure. Thus, distancing oneself became protection and self-sufficiency, a premature defense mechanism.

This logic doesn't end in childhood. On the contrary, it is reinforced and amplified by contemporary culture, which encourages emotional distancing for the sake of autonomy, productivity and individual life. We live pressured by ideas of achievement, by fragile narratives of "self-love", by utilitarian and disposable relations.

We learn to see the other either as a threat to our freedom or as the savior of our insecurities. Thus, at times we throw ourselves intensely onto the other in search of immediate security (the anxious pattern), and at other times we pull away at the exact moment intimacy threatens to break through our defenses (the avoidant pattern). The extremes feed each other, reinforcing a culture in which the fear of getting involved and the fear of being abandoned become confused, and the space of secure attachment—the space in which it is possible to trust, remain, and build together—becomes increasingly rare.

In the following chapters, we will explore how this logic manifests in the contemporary world: in romantic relationships, dating apps, social media, and even in the way we relate to time, the body, and affection. It is a complex question, a two-way street that moves from the individual to the collective, but also from the collective to the individual.

We created the culture we live in; therefore, the way we live as an individual affects the collective, in the same way we are affected by the culture that shapes how we feel and connect to one another. The individual and the collective are intertwined and reinforce one another with a precise logic, which we urgently need to rethink. Between excess and discard, there is an (in)evitable context. There is a culture and, why not say it, cultures.

Chapter 3

Julia's story

"Life is full of traces of what once was love
Sometimes, it isn't a big scene
It's the lip gloss forgotten in a pocket
A hummingbird print chosen with care when we bought it
The T-shirt left in the wardrobe
The bracelet with three knots and three wishes
A late-night dance in the kitchen
That book you suggested
The sculpture made with so much care
A special playlist you shared
That Backstreet Boys song we sang together in the car
Ice-skating hand in hand, laughing at how scared she was
Things that seem to be left behind
But love makes a home in the most ordinary things we find"
– **Danielle Vieira**

Let's talk about the story of someone I will call Julia. In this story, we will illustrate the bizarre manual of modern love and its unofficial instructions.

Julia, in her thirties, married young and stayed married for many years. She had been out of the dating scene; she came from a stable, beautiful, and healthy relationship, but one that ended, as any relationship can. After thinking it over for a few months, she felt ready to meet someone, and, at a friend's suggestion, decided to create a profile on a dating app.

She built an honest profile, chose beautiful photos, wrote a truthful and funny description, and was open to something new. Within two days, she had spoken to a few different men; two of them seemed very interested. One suggested a date and, on the day they were supposed to meet, canceled. The other was very excited to arrange a date for the following week, when he would be in town... and then he disappeared too. Meanwhile, many men sent messages, became excited about Julia, and when it was finally time to set up a date, everything cooled down and they stopped replying. Confused, Julia said to a friend: "I don't understand. We were talking all the time, the conversation was flowing well. Why do people disappear like that?"

Her friend, already a graduate of the dating-app school, answered with sad matter-of-factness: "Oh friend, it is just the way it is. They talk with many girls at the same time. And then, they hook up with whoever replies first, or whoever seems easier. It is like... an invisible championship. You only find out you lost when they stop talking to you. But sometimes they come back after a while; like on a Friday night, to see if you're available. Or sometimes they're just bored and want to talk, or say nonsense, just to get attention."

Julia laughed, because it was so absurd, but felt so real. Deep down, she did not want to compete with other people or have a collection of people to whom she could send messages; for her, it was not a game, it was about truly connecting with someone interesting, someone who could leave the virtual world and make the connection become something real.

When the first *match* became reality: "It is better to already have someone else on standby, in case this doesn't work out" ... "You have to go out with two or three people at the same time, so you can split your attention and not create expectations" ... That was the advice that Julia got when she said she was going out with the first *match* she got on a dating app.

Julia was confronted with what she called the "spare-tire logic" (keeping someone in reserve): you need to have someone on the bench in case the "current" one disappears, because then you will not suffer. But... Why can't we suffer anymore? Isn't that part of life? When did investing energy and time in someone become so out of style, to the point that we have to split our attention in little portions, so we don't get attached and suffer?

This notion of people as crutches, serving a purpose, whether to ease loneliness or fear, be a distraction or make you forget your ex, means that there will always be someone who will be useful and someone who will be discarded. In a society where everything must be functional all the time, people tend to become goods. We no longer relate to one another, we consume people... And, worse, we are consumed.

Julia carried on, believing that love was still possible, and found Romeo, her first match in real life, after two weeks texting they decided to meet. She was feeling super connected with the ideas and how easy their exchange was, things went better than expected; it really seemed that there was affinity and mutual desire there. They had five dates in five consecutive days, the conversation flowed, the chemistry was intense and so was the desire to repeat the dating experience.

Despite living in different countries, they decided to meet in another country halfway, in 10 days, so they could spend more time together. Julia was happy and open to whatever might happen. The date happened, everything was absolutely romantic, he took her to the top of a mountain to enjoy the view, they visited lakes and cities and they even went to a piano concert together! Passion began to knock at Julia's door, sparked by a surprise kiss she received on the Bridge of Love and by many other moments that felt like scenes from a Netflix romance. After five more days together, Romeo invited Julia to his country, to spend a few days there, get to know the city, and go on Christmas outings, since the end of the year was approaching and his city, at that time, was entirely lit up with Christmas markets.

Julia packed her bags. Ten days later they met again. He put together an itinerary with eleven Christmas markets because he knew how much Julia loved them. They shared intimacy, unique moments, and everything seemed to be moving in a direction in which both felt good in each other's presence and wanted more. The conversation was fun, chemistry remained intense, hugging was relaxing, they were very much in sync, traveling together was easy; both managed somehow to have similar ideas about the little things of daily life and they also could hold deeper conversations about life. There, they had that important conversation: he asked Julia where she thought the relationship was going. Julia said that they had two possibilities, they could decide to be together and would have to figure out how to make it work, given the distance. Or they could fall in love with someone else and life would keep going. But he said he was happy that they were taking things forward and then gave Julia a gift: his T-shirt, the one she had liked and decided to wear the night before. Julia was happy and saw the gesture as something symbolic and important, but it was already time to pack her bags and go home.

They agreed to meet again. And this time, the period would be longer, and in Julia's country. She was also excited to return, since she had been living abroad for a few years and longed to see her family and friends. But Julia also felt insecure, not knowing whether something so strong, yet still so new, could survive time.

During the two months that followed, he did not fail to text her, not even a single day. He told her about his adventures, sent photos, asked about her, made plans for the meeting and was very consistent. During this time, they fed many expectations, laughs, and hopes. Julia prepared a special trip through her country; they decided to spend twenty days together. The meeting finally happened. The wait was long, but not as long as the first kiss at the airport, or the first nights together after so much time waiting for that moment.

The first days were intense. They enjoyed the city and the typical parties of that time of the year and, on the fifth day, Julia noticed that he was different: he avoided looking into her eyes and there was a certain physical and emotional distance. She asked then what was going on, because she felt something was different, although she did not know exactly what it was. He said he was afraid of hurting her, because he did not want a serious relationship. He had decided that for his life, but he could see that she imagined that possibility. Julia said yes, that for her this was possible, but that she was not asking for it at that moment. She added that they had already had a certain conversation about it before and that, apparently, they had been on the same page.

Julia was confused, because he had never said he made that decision for his life.

Julia took a deep breath, did not spiral, and, without understanding much, decided to ask a few questions: why had he gone all the way there and nurtured the connection for five months if he had already made this life decision? After all, this was not a casual encounter, but a flight of more than ten hours for both of them, and a trip planned for two months so they could stay together for twenty days. He didn't quite know how to answer, and tried to justify himself with answers such as "I don't want to lose my freedom", "I don't want to have to ask for me-time", "I wouldn't be in a relationship with someone who doesn't speak my language", even though they both spoke English fluently with each other, and so on. They still had 15 days of their trip ahead. After one or two days, Julia asked whether he was uncomfortable and wanted to leave. He said no, that he wanted to stay and that he liked her.

Julia was confused and questioned herself: "If he likes me and says he does, if he makes the effort for me, if he nurtured this relationship, said he missed me and even joked around saying he was mine and that he had accepted his fate, if we had a real possibility of being together, why did he change his mind just like that, all of a sudden? Is it fear? Is he a Hollywood actor and faked it all? Was I really that naïve?"

Julia's dilemma is not hers alone. What appears to be a personal impasse, during a meeting awaited for months, and a potential love interrupted by fragile justifications, is, without a doubt, an individual symptom, but also a social one. What is at stake is not only what he feels or avoids feeling, or the fear of commitment, but a larger logic that cuts across contemporary relationships: the "I don't want to hurt you" that sounds more like "I don't want to implicate myself"... even though I am already implicated up to the neck!

Modern bonds have become bonds of convenience, not bonds of commitment. In fact, commitment has become "Voldemort," the most feared word of the moment, the name that must not be spoken.

It is possible to be in a "situationship"[4] that has everything a real relationship has, except for the name. It is a nameless situation: not boyfriend or girlfriend, not exclusive, not together; but not apart either; (almost) always together, with intense exchanges, affectively connected, spooning at night, going for walks in the morning, dating regularly, having intimacy, traveling together... But it is not a serious relationship. Do you get it? Neither did Julia.

Back when Julia was single, before the marriage, there was such a thing as a casual partner, or the "hookup", when we had just started to meet someone and would hook up with that person. Naturally, it could either evolve into a relationship or not, but it had a certain expiration date and, usually, led to being boyfriend/girlfriend; it was the rehearsal of a relationship. Today, no. This can last for months, years even, and never become something more, plus, usually, you can't even ask "what

> **POSSIBLE LOVE**
>
> Possible love does not happen instantly; bonds are not born ready-made. They are built and constantly shaped.

4 Situationship is an informal relationship, between friendship and serious dating, characterized by emotional and/or physical intimacy, with no explicit commitment. It is a form of connection between two people who do not consider themselves a couple, but have the routines of a couple, usually with no clear expectations about the future.

are we?"; that is forbidden language. Just let it follow the flow, without worrying too much about "labels."

In modern logic, bonds have become something like bottles of jam on a supermarket shelf: we compare the ingredients, the sizes, the prices and then we choose. If we don't like it, we throw it away, we test another one, often without even explaining why. People just disappear, the famous *ghosting*.[5]

In the culture of disposability, the logic is: if you do not like it, replace it. There is always someone better. Funnier. More beautiful. More interesting.

Apps designed to refine choices make people become profiles, serve a function, and fulfill a list of requirements: "This one is pretty, but not tall; this one is interesting, but doesn't want to have kids; this one smokes; this one has dogs; this one has cats; this one has children; this one doesn't have…"

The connection becomes a mathematical equation, impossible to be solved.

Some unofficial rules are: you can't say "Hi, how are you?" in the first message, because this is too boring. You need to be deep or funny in the very first sentences, otherwise it already feels like a job interview.

"Ugh, I can't be bothered to reply"… There is no time to lose. The first conversation must be like juggling and

5 Ghosting: means cutting off communication with someone entirely, with no explanations, as if the person had disappeared or become a ghost. It is more usual in romantic relationships, but can also happen in friendships and in the work environment.

the first date has to be magical; chemistry must happen in the very first touch. No room for boredom. No affective patience, nor the will to build a relationship.

In the culture of excess, the logic is to collect people instead of truly connecting, like in a menu, where we can choose "today's special." This leads us, inevitably, to a certain affective saturation, because there are a lot of stimuli, a lot of people, too many conversations, too many almosts and too little depth; too many new beginnings, which become exhausting, because of the high turnover they demand.

And when everything seems so disposable and easy, why invest in something that could last?

Investing takes too much work, it brings frustrations, misunderstandings, constant adjustments of route and perspective, recognition of one's own flaws and the need to evolve in order to continue. In other words, it requires leaving the comfort zone.

The idea that love has to be easy, light and fun all the time has gained too much strength. But... Love is not magic, and even less a perfect fit. Remaining in the bond of a possible love is making a choice, every day, despite everything; and a secure bond can only be born and survive if there is time, affective patience, the courage to choose to build something more meaningful, and a willingness to work on oneself and together.

For those who are afraid to feel, what is frightening is presence. And in the age of ghosting, presence can be synonymous with true love.

Julia's story could be the story of Maria, Sarah, John, Bruno, and the story of many people around the world who live balancing themselves between the excess of options and the speed of disconnection, promoting the culture of disposability and opening space for the culture of detachment, a new form of "avoidant love," which we will see next.

Chapter 4

Detachment culture

"Descartes, following the Stoics, has given a name to this possibility, which human reality has, to secrete a nothingness which isolates it—it is freedom."
– **Jean-Paul Sartre, French philosopher (Being and Nothingness).**

The concept of freedom has oscillated between poles from Antiquity to the present day. Freedom directly related to the individual is something relatively new; in Western culture, the concept of freedom was previously connected to collective action, moving through distinct poles at different moments in history. In Ancient Greece, for example, the Brazilian jurist Pansieri[6] reminds us that the truly free person was expected to participate in public life, in the political field, and to exercise citizenship ethically ("man is a political animal")[7]; the good life could only be fulfilled in the public sphere, reconciling democracy and aristocracy as mixed regimes.

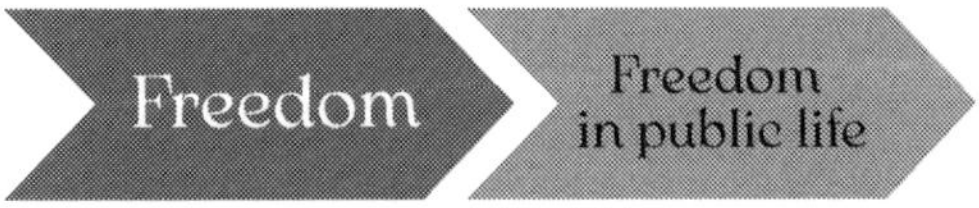

6 Pansieri, 2017.

7 Aristotle, Politics, I.2.

After the Macedonian conquests and Roman domination over the Greek city-states, freedom—previously connected to the exercise of politics—gave way to the concept of interiority, which was redefined by Stoicism. Authors such as Seneca and, later, Marcus Aurelius, affirmed that the free person was the one who mastered his passions and lived according to reason and the acceptance of life's circumstances.

Epictetus, who was a slave, sought to change his life through the concept of inner freedom, teaching that true freedom does not come from external circumstances, but from how we react to them, through self-control and discipline. This transition paved the way for the Christian synthesis that would follow.

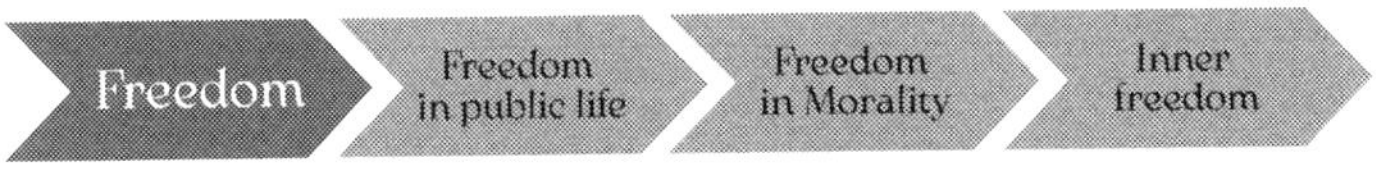

In the medieval period, Augustine of Hippo, also known as Saint Augustine (possibly one of history's first psychoanalysts without a divan), with his work *Confessions*, formulated the theory of illumination, and established the concept of free will, according to which man is free when he chooses, by his own free will, to follow the will of God (*De libero arbitrio*). Of course, here we need to consider the religious context to which Augustine belonged, but his ideas were not limited to religion and transcended into philosophy and psychoanalysis. In the perspective inaugurated by Saint Augustine, as the Brazilian jurist Tomasevicius Filho observes[8], freedom became an option through which the human being determines his own path, whose parameters of choice would be delimited by an external order that establishes the value or disvalue of each option.

According to him, to be free is not simply to do whatever one wants, but to will the good: the will only finds rest when it turns toward God. Thus, the Christian paradox is born: "free is the one who serves the other." In other words, freedom is fulfilled only in commitment, in a bond that, far from being slavery, is adherence to truth. It is worth emphasizing that Augustine lived a life in struggle with his own desires, experiencing for many years what he called "sins of the flesh" before becoming a religious man, and that the creation of his philosophy is directly connected to these experiences of extreme freedom, discipline, and renunciation. In this sense, his conception of free will is inseparable from the biographical experience that led him to understand that true freedom is not found in the satisfaction of desires, but in the orientation of the will toward the good and toward God.

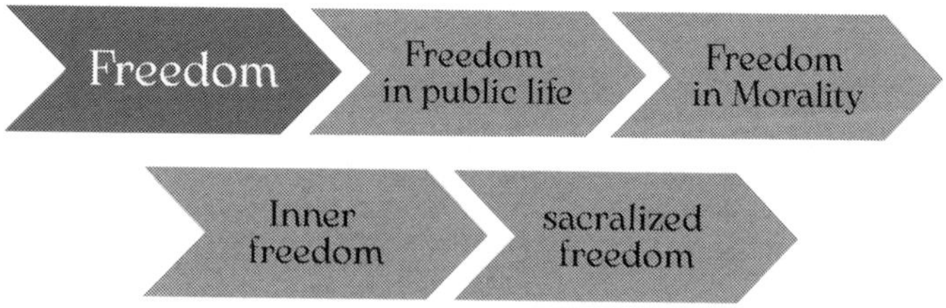

8 Tomasevicius Filho, 2006

Centuries later, in another register, Hegel would transform this question into a historical drama. In Phenomenology of Spirit (1807), the master-slave dialectic shows that freedom does not exist in an isolated form: it can only confirm itself in reciprocal recognition. The master, apparently free, depends on the slave in order to be recognized; the slave, in turn, through his relationship with work and with reality, conquers a more solid form of freedom. There is a master because there is a slave, and there is a slave because there is a master. Freedom is never absolute; it is born from the dialectic between master and slave and is realized in the recognition of the other. It depends on the gaze, the response, and the mediation of another, and therefore I am never entirely master of myself.

The French psychoanalyst Jacques Lacan[9] borrows this idea from Hegel and transports it into the field of desire when he says the famous phrase: "Desire is the desire of the Other." It seems like he is trying to explain to us, mere mortals, that what we desire does not come from within us as something natural; in other words, we learn to desire through the other's desire. Desire is the

9 Lacan, 1998.

fruit of culture, of the family environment, and of all the others who shape us. Thus, we grow up constantly trying to decipher what the other wants from us, what would make us lovable, accepted, recognized, so that we may know something about the other's desire and, in turn, may desire and be desired as well. The relationship between master and slave is grounded in recognition through work, through history. In Lacan, the dialectic is the unconscious and language. The Hegelian master and slave want to be recognized as free, while the Lacanian subject wants to be desired. In both cases, the truth is that the so-called freedom to be or to desire is always crossed, at best, by a structural dependence.

Well, if my desire is the desire of the Other and my freedom depends on the recognition of the Other, there is always a lack; I can never be sufficient, not even when I believe I am free, nor when I believe something is what I truly desire. Who is this thing called I, after all?

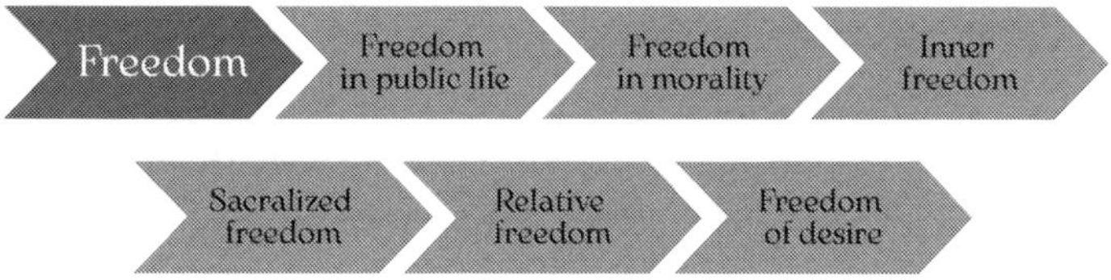

Jean-Paul Sartre, French philosopher, writer, and playwright, one of the leading names of twentieth-century existentialism, said: "Descartes, following the Stoics, has given a name to this possibility, which human reality has, to secrete a nothingness which isolates it—it is freedom." The expression "to secrete a nothingness which isolates it"

is a literary construction that evokes a profound meaning about the human condition. At its core, the phrase suggests the idea that the individual, through an internal action or a posture of inertia, produces the emptiness or absence that distances him from others and from the world. The person secretes (produces, creates) the nothingness (the absence of connection, affection, or purpose) that isolates him. Instead of being isolated by external factors, he himself creates the conditions for solitude. This passivity (the nothingness) becomes a barrier that distances him from others. And worse: he calls this condition freedom.

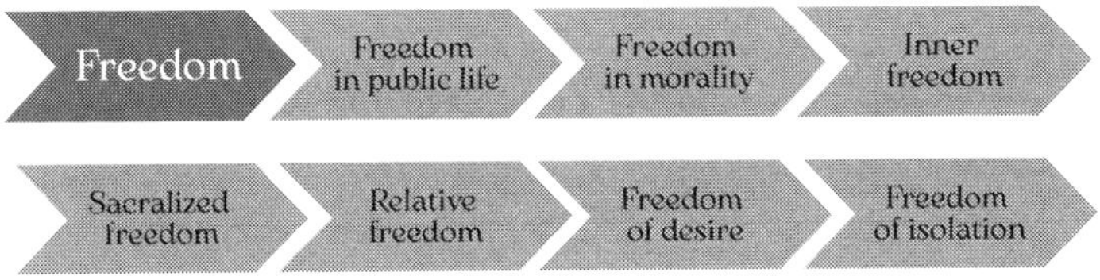

This is where modern culture enters, to redefine desire and freedom, with the proposal of putting an end to the anguish of having to deal with lack, because the basic principle of advertising is that there is someone who knows what we desire and promises that, once we possess a given object, we will be satisfied. But not only that: culture begins to sell the experience of being free.

And the generation that may have been most captured by this idea is the so-called millennials, those born from the mid-1980s to the end of the 1990s—and, quite possibly, the generations that followed as well (I open a parenthesis here, because I am not an anthropologist and do not conduct research in this field, but I am speaking from the clinical experience, through which we may have a sample, however small).

Previous generations cultivated a sense of freedom still closely related to leaving their parents' home for the commitment of marriage, dedication to family bonds, and the formation of a solid career that would guarantee financial stability. The idea of freedom could be directly attached to the idea of stability, which necessarily implied making bonds, establishing relationships (even if not very good ones), and creating networks that sustained a certain level of autonomy.

Contemporary culture began to commercialize experiences of freedom. We began to go farther, with planes, trains, and transportation infrastructure growing more and more each day. Globalization brought the incredible possibility of crossing borders, and tourism became massive and even a major problem in many European cities, for example. Driven even more by post-pandemic digital life, the motto "live life to the fullest," "travel without limits," "work from wherever you want" also fit with the dynamic of "date without commitment"; slogans that update, in everyday life, the old promise of full autonomy. It is freedom no longer as the formation of bonds, but as disconnection, detachment. With this, we created the illusion that we can live without depending, without making concessions, without allowing ourselves to be affected.

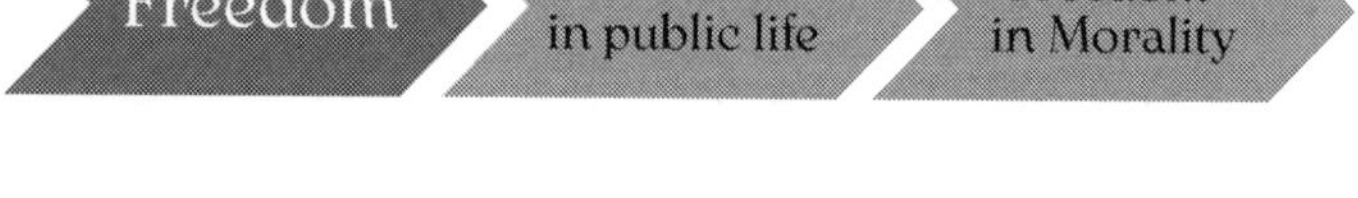

The word attachment comes from the verb to attach, from the Old French *attachier*, meaning to fasten, join, or bind. It carries the idea of something that holds, connects, ties, or clings. Detachment is precisely the negation: the act of releasing oneself, unsticking, coming apart. A quick search online is enough to find books that teach how to detach in relationships; how not to let yourself be affected; how to learn infallible methods to forget someone; how not to care.

The concept of detachment has expanded beyond "letting things flow," far beyond the Stoic principle of trusting and accepting what life brings; it has become a practice of emotional disengagement.

In the film Ghosts of Girlfriends Past (2009), Connor Mead (Matthew McConaughey) is a womanizing photographer who runs from commitment and takes pride in detachment. Right in the beginning, he says the following line: "Someone once told me that the power in all relationships lies with whoever cares less, and he was right. But power is not happiness, and I think that maybe happiness comes from caring more about people, not less."

The line summarizes the central conflict of the movie: the belief that detachment grants power, based on the idea that whoever feels less suffers less, set against the discovery that true happiness can only emerge when we allow ourselves to be affected, when we care more, not less. The character, a convinced bachelor who has left broken hearts along the way, is then revisited by the ghosts of his ex-girlfriends, in a kind of pedagogical journey that forces him to face his own past and learn about himself through the dynamics of relationships. And he understands that his behavior is nothing more than a defense against his own pain.

If Hegel shows us that freedom depends on the other, and Lacan reveals that desire is the desire of the Other, detachment emerges as the perfect strategy to deny a dependence that is constitutive. "I don't need anyone," "I don't get attached," "I am free because I don't depend"—contemporary mantras that try to silence the structural anguish of lack and, ultimately, of helplessness. Let us say that, perhaps, we have created a bad but very attractive solution to a nearly inevitable problem.

In recent years, the word dependence has taken on an almost always negative connotation, associated with fragility, submission, or pathology. We speak of emotional dependence as if it were a deviation, something to be cured so that the subject may return to being fully autonomous and free.

It is true that there are people who suffer from pathological dependence and cannot sustain their own lives without someone else, living in suffering or even in abusive relationships, because they believe they are only allowed to exist if the other is there to validate them, to see them or sustain their identity (often fragile and filled with traumatic experiences). What we will approach here is how these concepts get intertwined and place us in a position of confusion between the extremes

- Pathological dependence;
- Fear of dependence;
- Extreme detachment.

We have forgotten, and perhaps have not even realized, that there is something between these three concepts, something Winnicott calls **relative dependence**.

Relative dependence is a sustainable form of dependence, which does not imply fusing with one another, but is also not such that we are completely detached, disconnected from the other.

In this model of dependence, identity and individuality are preserved and sustained, but they are also affected by the other. It's that familiar saying "you can be you", "I can be me" and, together, we can create a "we." And as I write, I have in my mind the image of two threads, each one a different color, and a knot, where the two individualities become intertwined. And, even mixed together, you can see which thread is blue and which one is green. There is no fusion; there is interaction, coming together, there is closeness, there is contour, new drawings, there is beauty; but each one with their own color.

Freedom in relationships always touches the fear of dependence, it gives rise to a tension that is seen as a threat, because "to what extent can I love and be loved without losing myself?" In this sense, is detachment really freedom, or merely a defense against the anguish of lack, rejection, and abandonment? How can we find a balance between a strengthened self, but not an individualistic and selfish one, that allows itself to affect and be affected, but does not lose itself in the other or because of the other?

These are reflections of our time, for which we may not yet have answers, but which lead us toward possible paths in possible love: a love in which avoidance, before turning into action, passes through honest and conscious reflection.

AVOIDANCE

Chapter 5

In love or addicted to you?

"There is always some madness in love. But there is also always some reason in madness."
– **Friedrich Nietzsche**

We are beings of language, filled with considerably complex emotions and small existential dilemmas that haunt us quite often; in addition, we are also little walking cocktails of neurotransmitters and chemicals that rule the show behind the scenes.

We can write poems, compose songs, swear eternal love or philosophize about freedom, but all it takes is a couple of agitated molecules in the brain to turn a nice dinner into a declaration of love or a jealousy fit; a romance into a breakup; a passion into obsession; an intense desire into absolute silence. In short: we are extremely sophisticated creatures and, yet, paradoxically, we function like a little chemical pinball machine running at full speed, with side effects called love, passion, addiction, and drama (not necessarily in that order).

These substances, called neurotransmitters, are responsible for carrying messages to and from our nervous system and, whenever we experience feelings, sensations, and emotions, we are also being governed by this intense chemistry, that takes place silently.

The neuroscience researcher Larry Young, coauthor of the book *The Chemistry Between Us: Love, sex and the science of attraction*, published in 2012 with the journalist Brian Alexander[10], defends the idea that love is not only an irrational mystery, nor can it be reduced to biology, but there is a bridge between biology and human experience, and understanding the chemistry behind love doesn't mean reducing that mystery to something purely biological, and vice-versa… On the contrary: understanding both contexts can help us gain more clarity about how these mechanisms operate when we begin to feel interested in someone, why we feel drawn to that particular person, and why we activate not-so-healthy mechanisms that make us confuse love with addiction.

The author's research shows that attraction is not as random as it seems. There is a hormone dance and subtle signs that influence our choices, such as the tendency women have, during ovulation, of feeling attracted to confident, dominant men, the so-called "bad boys." In studies with strippers, those who were ovulating received more tips and the clients, even without knowing, responded to these subtle signs of fertility. In other words, we are not so much in control over our choices as we think, which is why we'll explore some of the chemistry behind love and infatuation, so we can better understand our emotions and affections.

---

10 Young, L.; Alexander, B, 2012.

Dopamine

It all begins with dopamine, the molecule of seeking, a neurotransmitter our neurons use to communicate with one another. When we lock eyes with someone who attracts us, or when we begin to get involved with someone who awakens "that something more" in us, the hypothalamus sends signals that flood the nucleus accumbens with dopamine and adrenaline. This part of the brain is also known as the pleasure center. The nucleus *accumbens* is an area of the brain that works as an interface between motivation and action, and it is crucial to systems of reward, pleasure, and motivation.

Dopamine is closely connected to the feeling of euphoria that moves our motivation and reward system. It is a neurotransmitter that makes us seek pleasure, whether connected to food, sex, drugs, music, or that person who attracts us. We think we want them as much as we would want a drug, as if we could no longer live without them.

This is why, when we fall in love with someone, we have the feeling of being addicted. The first stages are a kind of endogenous intoxication: endless energy, obsessive focus, euphoria that results in endless text messages, stalking social media, thinking about the person all day, a need to be close, intense physical intimacy, and other forms of madness that passion provides.

Larry Young[11] points out, in his research, that rats separated from their mating partners present signs of withdrawal very similar to those of users deprived of cocaine. Science confirms what the Greeks already knew: the origin of the Greek word *pathos (πάθος)*, which means suffering and which is, to a certain extent, pathological. This is why passion resembles addiction so closely: the body reacts as if it had just ingested a stimulant substance. The increase in dopamine at the beginning of a relationship is so intense that some scientists compare passion to a state of temporary intoxication.

Dopamine represents the arriving novelty, the *like*, the *reels*, the reaction to *stories*, all interactions on social media in general, the unexpected message that arrives and makes us feel like we have butterflies in our stomach. But, contrary to what people think, this neurotransmitter is more connected to anticipation than to pleasure. And when this becomes excessively connected within our system, the brain compensates with discomfort, leading to a tolerance that demands increasingly stronger stimuli to reach the same level of satisfaction.

Curiously, while dopamine rises, serotonin plummets. This is why someone in love behaves like someone with a mild OCD (obsessive-compulsive disorder): intrusive thoughts, a need for constant contact, anxiety when the other person does not reply. The entire brain screams: "Go

---

11 Larry Young (1967–2024) was a US neuroscientist who held the William P. Timmie Chair in Translational Neuroscience at the Department of Psychiatry, School of Medicine of Emory University.

after them, don't let them get away!" The post-dopamine emptiness is real and, by itself, makes us insatiable, excites us, and has an ephemeral duration. We are always searching, and the more we receive the reward, the more we want to keep searching.

This mechanism, which once served survival, in the actions of hunting, eating, and looking for partners, is now also exploited by consumer culture and the attention economy. Social media, pornography, ultra-processed foods, online shopping, and even dating apps continuously activate dopamine. The result is a kind of loop of infinite seeking, in which we are never satisfied for very long. In love, this translates into disposable relationships, the addiction to collecting people instead of truly connecting, the need for constant novelty, and the difficulty of sustaining bonds once the initial euphoria fades.

The psychiatrist Anna Lembke, in her book, *Dopamine Nation: Finding Balance in the Age of Indulgence*, expands this discussion, by showing that even the circuit that makes us love also puts us at risk in a world of hyperstimulation. Pleasure and pain are processed in the same neural systems, and every spike of pleasure generates a counterweight in the direction of pain. As the author says, "We've transformed the world from a place of scarcity to a place of overwhelming abundance."[12] Everything is designed to give us pleasure and, paradoxically, we end up in a state of constant dissatisfaction.

---

12 Lembke, 2021.

This would explain why every excess has a price: the more we search for intense stimuli, the more the brain creates tolerance and demands higher doses to achieve the same effect.

The personal and social price of being ruled by the next "dose" of dopamine invites us to find a healthier balance between pleasure and pain in modern life.

Oxytocin

But the euphoria of dopamine does not last forever or, at least, it should not. Our body enters a state of stress, cortisol rises, and we cannot handle this dopaminergic overdose for too long.

If dopamine drives us in the beginning and moves us toward someone, oxytocin, together with vasopressin, establishes the bonds between two people: mother and baby, lovers, friends. The American researcher Sue Carter was one of the pioneers that showed that oxytocin, traditionally associated only with childbirth and breastfeeding, has a much wider role in social and emotional life. In her 2014 article, "Oxytocin Pathways and the Evolution of Human Behavior", Carter sums up decades of research and suggests that the systems regulated by oxytocin and vasopressin were key for the evolution of human behavior.[13]

It is that invisible thread that connects all of us: the bonding hormone, the smell, the touch, the hug, the

13 Carter, 2014.

look, that makes you feel and gives meaning to it all. They are small molecules, but very powerful. Released especially through physical contact, such as childbirth, breastfeeding, hugs, and sex, they glue people to one another, connecting directly to the nucleus *accumbens* and the amygdala. Nature does not waste energy: if so much time is spent finding a partner, it is necessary to ensure that the bond is reinforced. Oxytocin and vasopressin increase trust, reduce fear, and create the feeling of a certain establishment of bond.

Studies with rodents help to illustrate this biological facet: some rodents in North America, known as prairie voles, are strictly monogamous. When analyzed, it was discovered that the brains of these animals are full of oxytocin and vasopressin receptors in the reward areas. Mountain voles, on the other hand, with fewer oxytocin receptors, do not have an exclusive partner and live with several partners. When scientists blocked these hormones in the monogamous voles, they became indifferent to their partners, suggesting that oxytocin plays an important role not only in remaining together, but also in these animals' fidelity. In humans, intranasal oxytocin, in experiments, made men find their partners more attractive, not just any woman, but the partners with whom they were in a relationship.

Carter showed that the density and the distribution of these receptors vary from individual to individual, influenced by genetic and epigenetic factors. This variation helps explain why some people create lasting bonds more easily, while others show greater difficulty in establishing stable relationships.

A central point in her theory is the role that oxytocin plays in the evolution of human sociality. The author suggests that not only the molecule made prolonged maternal care possible, which is essential for highly dependent offspring such as human offspring, but also contributes to the expansion of the social brain. By regulating physiological processes such as stress and oxygenation during childbirth, oxytocin would have allowed both encephalization and the increasing complexity of the social bonds that characterize our species.

The research also highlights the effects of oxytocin on the autonomic nervous system and the stress axis. Under favorable conditions, its action reduces fear, anxiety, and hostility, promoting approach and a sense of safety. But Carter reminds us that these effects are not universal; everything depends on the social context and on each individual's life history. Early experiences, such as the maternal bond, or stressful situations in childhood, can alter the expression of oxytocin receptors and shape social sensitivity throughout life.

All of this means that the biology of bonding is not something fixed, but rather plastic and characterized by the interaction between environment and organism, and that although science has advanced a lot on this subject, there are still more questions than answers about such a complex mechanism. But one question deserves our reflection: how conscious are we of this integrative factor in the development of our relationships today?

Serotonin

Dopamine is what makes us seek and oxytocin is responsible for bonding. Serotonin, on the other hand, is the neurotransmitter that stabilizes: it is the calm after the storm. It is responsible for regulating mood, sleep, and the sensation of well-being. When this hormone is well adjusted, we have the feeling of balance.

Several studies suggest that, during the phase of falling in love, serotonin levels in the brain tend to drop. This reduction is associated with what we have already described as intrusive thoughts, idealization, anxiety, and that feeling of "I can't stop thinking about this person." In biological terms, the person in love and the patient with obsessive-compulsive disorder (OCD) share the same kind of pattern: a brain taken over by repetitive circuits.

Psychologist and researcher Sandra Langeslag reviewed a series of studies that confirm this effect.[14] People in love show reduced

> **POSSIBLE LOVE**
>
> Healthy life experiences and interactions can influence the production of these hormones, reinforcing positively our capacity to create and maintain secure relationships.

14 Langeslag, 2009.

levels of serotonin in the blood and a lower density of transporters of this substance, the same transporters that regulate the neurotransmitter's availability in the brain. A classic study, conducted by Donatella Marazziti in 1999, showed that in individuals at the height of passion, the density of the serotonin transporter (SERT) was as low as in patients with OCD and that, about a year later, when the phase of passion had calmed down, these levels returned to normal.

Other studies confirm this pattern. An Indian study[15] observed that people who fell in love more easily presented lower levels of serotonin than those involved in arranged marriages, where the bond is created without the euphoria phase. A clinical report from Walsh and Bitner (2006) describes a patient that, after using selective serotonin reuptake inhibitors (SSRIs), reported experiencing love in a shorter and more lukewarm way, as if the excess of serotonin blocked the vertigo that characterizes falling in love. There is also evidence that genetic factors modulate this system. Studies with the serotonin 2A receptor gene (5-HT2A) have associated certain genetic variations with a more possessive and impulsive type of love, one that borders on obsession and dependency. This same receptor is involved in aggressive and impulsive behaviors, which helps explain why some people, when faced with romantic rejection, oscillate between idealization and loss of control.

---

15 Kurup & Kurup, 2003.

The general hypothesis is that the serotonergic system changes only in the early stages of passion, gradually returning to balance as love matures.

When the dopamine levels drop and oxytocin begins to dominate, serotonin rises again, allowing the bond to become more stable. It is at this point that love stops being a roller coaster of emotions and becomes a calmer and safer space.

But balance comes at a price. As the brain restores normal serotonin levels, we also lose part of the initial excitement. This is the moment when reality imposes itself: the other person is no longer fully idealized, flaws appear, and the relationship must now be sustained not by obsession, euphoria, and passion, but by the real combination that contains both the good and the bad. And perhaps this is where the challenge of modern relationships lies, since everything around us has been programmed to activate our dopaminergic system and make us feel pleasure.

The equation of love could be translated as

Permanence

Stimulus + Dopamine + Oxytocin + Serotonin + Presence + Time

The equation that we created for modern love, on the other hand:

Cyclic

Stimulus + Dopamine + Excitement + Oxytocin + Fear + Flight

Are we living a dilemma between biology and culture? On one side, we have the intrinsic need for bonding and relationality; on the other, culture shapes us to escape and seek more pleasure at any cost.

Could neuroplasticity, that is, our capacity to be shaped in response to the environment, be modified by our hyperconnected and dopaminergic contemporary lifestyle?

The search engine is also, in the final analysis, an addiction engine. It awakens the thrill of the hunt. And perhaps the great challenge of modern love is no longer to seek the ideal partner, or even to find love, but to deepen relationships when everything around us calls us back to the surface.

Chapter 6

The superficiality of modern love

"All art is characterized by a certain mode of organization around this emptiness."
– **Jacques Lacan**

On some ordinary day, a few years ago, I decided to go to the movies to watch *A Star Is Born*, in the version starring Lady Gaga and Bradley Cooper. I went without much expectation, because I like the actors and music, and it seemed to be a very musical film. I remember that, at that moment, I was in a sensitive phase of my life, and the film touched me in a way that, to this day, I still cannot quite explain, but I left the cinema absolutely disturbed. I cried from the beginning to the very end—and for the rest of the evening. I asked myself what it was about that movie that moved me so intensely, or whether it was me who was kind of unhinged; maybe a little bit of both, but I noticed that other people were also there at the end wiping their tears away, trying to recompose themselves. I realized that the movie speaks about something very complex—about human emotions in a love relationship undermined by psychological suffering—in a relatively simple yet poetic way, one that felt intensely familiar. After all, as it goes in that famous phrase attributed to

Freud: "Everywhere I go, I discover that a poet has been there before me." It is in art that an immeasurable field of wisdom resides... The field of affections!

The main soundtrack, written by Lady Gaga, opens with a question that challenges listeners to examine whether they have found genuine happiness in the modern world, or whether they are merely exhausting themselves trying to fill an inner void. The chorus arrives as a declaration that love has carried the protagonists beyond shallowness and into depth. Indeed, the film is marked by a certain intensity, from the interaction between the actors and the eye-to-eye scenes, which seem to last for hours, to the soundtrack, produced by Lady Gaga herself, and which embodies the movie's message in a brilliant way.

Some time later, in Brazil, the version of the main song was adapted by singer Paula Fernandes and, curiously, the lyric, instead of being "We are far from the shallow now," was remodeled as "Juntos e shallow now," which means "together and shallow now," ironically giving the opposite meaning of the original lyric and of the film's proposal, but, in a certain way, a kind of Freudian slip that works very well to illustrate and reflect a little of modern relationships.

Shallowness seems to be more connected to the inability, or the choice, not to go deeper into complex themes, such as affection and bonds; it is intimately linked to the way we relate to something or to someone. Ultimately, shallowness seems to be a symptom that protects us from complex affections and preserves a certain autonomy and a relative "peace".

The shallowness of relationships seems to be the formula of modern love, where we find a way of having or simulating a connection with the other without being in fact able to sustain the complexity of such connection. In this new way of having relationships without ever going into depth in them, one is present only to the bare minimum without exposing oneself too much; it is a certain way of playing safe that preserves the feeling of control and avoids the tension of what the psychoanalyst Jessica Benjamin calls mutuality.

For Benjamin, every encounter between two people is born from a tension between self-affirmation (desire for autonomy) and recognition (openness to the other). Coming back to Hegel's idea (that was already explored by other authors such as Lacan and Winnicott), there is an intense conflict between the desire to be recognized, the desire to dominate and also the desire to avoid dependency or submission.

If we go back a little in history, Winnicott had already brought to us this brilliant idea that the baby only acquires the feeling of being real if it finds a "good-enough" environment, that is, an "other" who recognizes it as such. But it is not any other. Benjamin reinforces this idea that the other has to be a subject with value on their own, and not just a mirror reflecting validation back to us. For this recognition to be authentic, the other must assert themselves as distinct from us, in an operation that inevitably involves a certain degree of negation or differentiation. It is precisely there that the paradox resides: whoever searches for recognition must also maintain their own autonomy, while whoever recognizes faces the dilemma of affirming themselves as a subject without renouncing the openness to the other. As Jessica Benjamin writes, "There are any number of near-synonyms for it: to recognize is to affirm, validate, acknowledge, know, accept, understand, empathize, take in, tolerate, appreciate, see, identify with, find familiar, ... love." And, with these few terms highlighted by her, we already have enough complexity for any relationship.[16]

This tension between the need for recognition and the affirmation of individuality creates a fragile and unstable balance. Small failures in mutual attunement, such as the irritation of an exhausted child or the withdrawal of an anxious, bored, or depressed mother, are enough to break this delicate thread. In these moments, not only does the symbolic play of the relationship come undone, but a kind of "anti-play" emerges, a small breakdown, in which the pain of nonrecognition becomes visible, almost palpable.

Like in this passage of the beautiful movie *Her*, from Spike Jonze, where the main character talks about his mother with Samantha, the artificial intelligence with whom he has a relationship: "My relationship with her was good...Well, actually, the thing I've always found frustrating about my mom is if I tell her something that's going on in my life, her reaction is usually about her..."[17]

---

16 Benjamin, 1988.

17 Her, dir. Spike Jonze, Warner Bros., 2013.

The cycle of affection and response can, then, become a spiral of mismatched encounters. The pain that comes from lack of recognition manifests itself as conflict: the relationship becomes a battlefield, a dispute for validation and domination, where every gesture can become the attempt to control or to run. Play becomes a field of tension, sometimes marked by the desire to get rid of the other and cancel out the connection, other times by an anxious fixation that prevents any healthy distance. One chases, the other withdraws. Frustration begins to dominate the space that once belonged to mutual exchange.

When these failures of mutuality repeat early on, they become deep affective marks. The child grows up without learning to enjoy the presence of the other with genuine pleasure, and without finding satisfaction in their own company either. They live between the fear of losing the bond and the inability to enjoy it.

This dynamic was identified by Winnicott, between the 1950s and 1960s, when observing patients who reported a kind of existential emptiness, a lack of vitality that seemed to have no evident cause. These individuals could not give meaning to their experiences, felt disconnected from life, living in a very superficial way, as if something essential had never been formed. Winnicott then began to investigate the obstacles to the constitution of a subjectivity capable of feeling pleasure, pain, and presence, someone who could develop the capacity to care about the other (concern), without being swallowed by the need for control or devoured by greed.

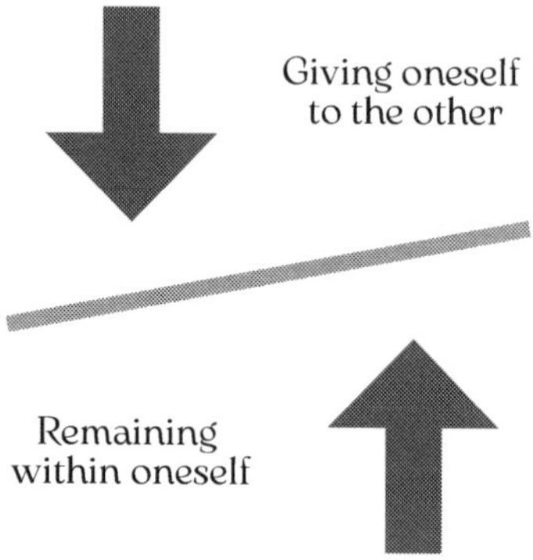

The hypothesis that emerges from these observations is that the first collapses of the experience of mutuality lie at the core of these disturbances. When the balance between giving oneself to the other and remaining within oneself is broken, a tension between submission and flight is installed.

The person oscillates between looking desperately for the gaze of the other and trying to protect themselves from it, losing the relational spontaneity.

The pleasure of emotional affinity, born from authentic exchange, gives way to dynamics of superiority, inferiority, rejection, or exclusion, experiences that weaken personal sovereignty and shake the narcissistic field of identity. Here, we can better understand why modern love has become a game of who cares less. Caring for the other demands the capacity to deal with complex feelings, but we keep reproducing, in a way, this game of recognition which becomes more and more narcissistic, driven by the overexposure of the curated self on social media

This type of suffering is increasingly common in clinical practice. It is not only the pain of rejection, but a certain anguish of not knowing or not being able to inhabit this "in-between" space, experiencing a series of missed connections, protected by bonds that remain on the surface precisely because they cannot move through, or rather sustain, this dilemma of mutuality.

Affective neoliberalism brings this logic turned toward the self, that we must "prioritize ourselves," "shield ourselves," "protect ourselves from bonds," and ends up reinforcing superficial and utilitarian relationships. The rupture of mutuality creates the illusion of a freedom that, deep down, is a negation of the other, out of fear of getting involved and being hurt. But not only that: it is also a fear of having to face up to our own emotional fragilities. It is a fear disguised as self-care, self-esteem, and self-worth. As Benjamin says: "The painful result of success in the battle for omnipotence is that to win is to win nothing: the result is negation, emptiness, isolation."[18]

In that regard, it seems that the superficiality of relationships brings us a certain apathy, an emotional anesthesia that protects us from something. And, for each person, this may be different. There is no conflict in shallowness; we can live according to the "Good Vibes Only" logic: we do not invoke a necessary capacity for internal transformation that requires effort and work, we do not have to face frustration (I mean… don't we?) and,

---

18 Benjamin, The Bonds of Love, p. 35.

ultimately, we don't deal with this pressure of having to dance to a choreography we don't know very well with another stranger, carried by a song whose rhythm, at times, we do not recognize.

Superficiality keeps us in control, but... perhaps it is in the choice of bonds, where we can practice alterity, that the true autonomy of being with the other is born. In the words of Brazilian psychoanalyst Joel Birman, "self-love would find a kind of relative balance with love for the other,"[19] and belonging would not directly conflict with being, allowing both to coexist.

I remember very well that, while in the middle of an argument with a very dear person, I heard the following question: "Aren't you the most important person in your life?" In that context, he used this to justify why he prioritized himself and only did what he wanted. And I answered: "Yes, but it's exactly because I know who I am and feel secure about it that I can put the other first; I don't have to worry about myself all the time." This sentence kept spinning in my head for days, until it brought me the thought: being sure of yourself and of your identity—and, in a way, being intimate with your own limits—does not mean putting yourself always first, but being able to take the other into consideration without annulling yourself and without constantly worrying about yourself. Sometimes, I prioritize myself, sometimes, I prioritize the other. And this seems to be one way out for a possible love.

19 Birman, 2016.

The dilemma here is not only superficiality with the other, but, ultimately, superficiality with ourselves. For many people who live constantly preoccupied with themselves, all the time, with their own image, performance, and control, there seems to be a great deficit of intimacy with their own feelings, with their desires, fears, and longings.

Perhaps one of the ways out toward a possible love is precisely to lose a little of oneself, in search of cultivating intimacy with the other.

Chapter 7

Intimacy deficit

"Because whoever loves never knows what they love
Nor knows why they love, or what loving is...
To love is eternal innocence
And the only innocence is not to think..."
– **Alberto Caeiro (heteronym of Fernando Pessoa)**

We all probably consume different kinds of podcast content on topics that interest us; besides being an excellent way to learn, there is also the entertainment aspect. One day, a psychiatrist was talking about how we are building an increasingly lonely, anxious, and disconnected generation, while also explaining the neuroscience behind attraction and attachment, teaching how to create connections that last, but what caught my attention the most in all that content was a comment from a random person that said something like: "We are all on our phones, watching videos about how to connect with other people, endlessly scrolling through videos of attractive girls/guys, adjusting our Tinder profiles, and overthinking all of it. For God's sake. Humanity is having an identity crisis." The lucidity of that comment is brutal.

Ironically, we are all searching for connection and, more and more, we are living through an intimacy deficit. We absorb internet content that teaches the science behind love, the chemistry, the strategies for a lasting relationship—things that seem to belong to an absolutely rational order—when, in truth, intimacy comes from somewhere else, somewhere that does not pass through analytical capacity.

> *One of the main factors in the creation of intimacy is spontaneity, curiosity, kindness, openness, and the acceptance of differences. And also time: intimacy is slow in a world that moves at a relentless pace.*

Today, contrary to what many people think, true intimacy does not come from sex or from being naked together; that has become a certain kind of routine and even something banal. Sex, which was once an expression of bond and mystery, has become a form of validation. The promise of sexual freedom, that seemed to free the body, created a new kind of coercion: one must always be available, desiring, performative. The body became a showcase, and pleasure became a product to be consumed, measured by intensity and novelty. The other is just a tool used to satisfy my own desire.

Physical contact has become very easy, but emotional encounter… increasingly rare. In the field of bonds, this dynamic frequently appears in avoidant attachment patterns. The subject seeks sex as a safe space because, within it, control seems possible; within it, one is allowed to let go, even if only sensorially, so that some emotion can flow before rational control takes over again. Everything happens too fast, with little room for imagination, for building intimacy. The contemporary imperative is to enjoy, not to relate. The result is a form of "sexual dictatorship": there is no longer repression of pleasure, but an obligation to experience it. The subject who does not feel desire or does not perform intensity is seen as abnormal.

Maybe true intimacy is not connected to sex anymore, but comes from a place that is both simpler and far more complex to reach, related to the capacity to abandon, at least a little, the analytical gaze, the obligations of performance, and to connect with the other in a vulnerable, spontaneous way. Sharing what is most intimate in us, what we always try to hide from others in order to appear self-sufficient, what reveals precisely that we are insufficient: our fears, our insecurities, our incoherences, our flaws; everything that takes us back to our small, helpless child-self, crying out for someone to see us, while at the same time not seeing us too much.

We fear revealing ourselves entirely, showing this other vulnerable part, because that would mean losing the other or losing the imaginary control we have over ourselves and over our Ego Ideal, as Winnicott stated: "It is a joy to be hidden, but a disaster not to be found."[20] And it seems that we live within this dynamic: on the one hand, hiding brings autonomy and freedom; on the other, not being found is a disaster, insofar as we are increasingly lonely and disconnected.

We are constantly confusing self-knowledge with self-love, but a selfish kind of self-love, one that runs away from the slightest discomfort in order to preserve a relative peace. And so, we hit loneliness once again.

20 Winnicott, 1963/1965, p. 186.

One of the most important things for growth, and what actually brings us some kind of development, is conflict. That old saying our grandparents used to repeat—"those who do not learn through love learn through pain"—may even be true, but suffering does not teach if we are not willing to learn. As the popular saying goes: "If suffering really taught, the world would be populated by wise people." Pain has nothing to teach those who do not find the courage and strength to listen to it. Those who are minimally conscious of themselves will see conflict as an opportunity for learning, resolution, confrontation, and doing things differently. But because, in general, we live in an avoidant modus operandi, most people avoid conflict in order to avoid the discomfort it brings, not only in relation to the other, but also in relation to themselves.

To avoid conflict is to avoid the encounter with what is most real in us: the uneasiness that, ultimately, points toward something more: our desires and our limitations. The frequent avoidant and anxious state in which we live makes us perceive, understand, and experience conflicts as threats. In the era of the situationship, one cannot demand, one cannot ask, one cannot create rules, one cannot create expectations, because all of this creates divergence, demand, and conflict. We prefer to lose someone rather than be honest about what we feel; we prefer to ghost, to disappear, rather than reveal that perhaps it is not the right moment, that we are afraid of getting involved, or that we have changed our mind about the relationship; because in love, and in relationships in general, it is necessary to recognize mutual difficulties and work on them.

We live in a cycle of self-deception, but avoiding a difficult conversation does not make the problem magically disappear; we merely "kick the can down the road", or as we say in Brazil, "push it with our belly", we postpone it, drag it along, leave it for later. And, most likely, we will repeat the same mistakes until we have enough courage to face the problem, or enough emotional maturity to sustain discomfort without running away.

Conflict avoidance is, in essence, a form of ego protection, but it comes at a high price. Many times, we avoid conflict in order to keep the other person close, and end up losing the bond because we do not know how to deal with conflict. This contradiction marks many contemporary relationships: people who prefer silence to clarity, distance to exposure, in a scenario where losing someone seems safer than being vulnerable.

A patient once asked me: "Why don't many men say *no*?"

This question often comes up in clinical practice and among female friends, especially when we talk about heterosexual relationships and certain patterns that appear in male behavior within affective dynamics. Of course, this does not apply to all men, nor only to men, but it is a recurring pattern worth observing. In some cases, men avoid directly ending relationships, even when they are no longer satisfied. Some disappear after showing interest, without explanations, without dialogue, without clear closure. Others maintain relationships out of inertia, without emotional presence, either to avoid the discomfort of confrontation or out of convenience, often because they have greater difficulty communicating what they are thinking or feeling.

There are some hypotheses regarding this question:

- From an early age, men learn to avoid difficult conversations that show vulnerability, especially those involving another person's emotional frustration.
- There is the fear of being the villain, the need to preserve their self-image, and the possibility of no longer being admired or desired if vulnerability is shown.
- Men have been taught, from early on, that they need to be strong, admired, and providers; they were educated to focus on the external world: achievements, possessions, material goods, etc. They were not taught that what most attracts the modern woman is not only strength, material goods, or professional success, but also someone who can deal with his own emotions and communicate them.

According to some studies, the skill most sought by women on dating apps is emotional intelligence. Most men today do not seem to have an affective vocabulary to know what they feel or what they want, which is also why they do not know how to communicate their feelings and desires. Besides that, in a world full of choices, it becomes increasingly difficult to take risks and make decisions, which leads to a certain emotional immaturity and to the preservation of superficiality as a defense, often combined with relationships that still offer some benefit, whether attention, affection, validation, sex, etc. So, they do not break up, they do not make a choice, and they are experts at leaving everything in a state of emotional ambiguity that is comfortable for them.

I am not saying that only men avoid conflict, because, in general, we live in an increasingly avoidant society (and I know men with high communication skills and emotional maturity), but it is important to recognize that the way boys and girls have been educated over decades directly influences the way men and women deal with emotions today. This difference in emotional socialization is reflected in affective behaviors and in the capacity to recognize, regulate, and communicate feelings in adult life.

One day, I was talking with a friend and I repeated this question: "Why do you think men don't break up?" He answered straightforwardly: "Because we always want to keep our options open." I think here we have precisely an answer that collaborates with a system in which love has been replaced by a management of possibilities. He does not want to be with someone, but wants to ensure that he could be, if he wanted to. And even when he does want to be with someone, he still wants to make sure he has more options in case the option of the moment goes wrong.

Within the dopamine logic, what matters is the game of conquest, a test to validate whether I'm still desired, even if in a childish and narcissistic way. Maintaining the other "available" preserves the illusion of control and avoids the risk of rejection. It is a dynamic that feeds on imbalance: the more available the other person appears, the less interesting they become; the more they withdraw, the more desire they generate. There is no real encounter, only the alternation between chase and flight. This modern game of ego validation is not born from pleasure, but from a strong and constant feeling of insecurity, even if veiled. Affection gives way to strategy, converted into a performance of efficiency, and, in this game, whoever shows less emotion wins. But wins what?

Intimacy is replaced by the management of one's own image and the love language is marked by economic terms. Intimacy, which demands time and continuity, becomes impossible in an environment that rewards strategy, acceleration and accumulation. This rationalization of affections impoverishes bonds, because love does not obey the law of equivalence, of fair exchange, all the time. On the contrary, love is the encounter between two different lacks, therefore irrational, as Lacan puts it well: "To love is to give what one doesn't have to someone who doesn't want it."[21]

POSSIBLE LOVE

The true love encounter seems to be the one that throws us off our center, breaks the continuity of the Ego and gives us back something that we didn't know about ourselves.

21 Lacan, The Seminar of Jacques Lacan, Book VIII: Transference, p. 34.

Under this premise, to love is not to be fulfilled by the other; it is to offer something we do not quite know what is, without guarantees that the other will give us the same measure in return, which involves risk and a great deal of courage (an absolutely scarce asset nowadays).

I am not saying that we must love someone who gives us nothing, but that, to some extent, there will always be dissonances in the capacity to give, in the way we show love, and in the way we love. There are days when love may be balanced and we give and receive in a more equivalent way, but there will be days when one person only has 20% to give, while the other will need to make a greater effort and complete the remaining 80%, and vice versa. If there is no willingness to move between giving and receiving in different measures, the relationship really does become a dispute and a territory of hypervigilance.

Breton writes in L'Amour fou (Mad Love): "It is really as if I had been lost and they had come to give me some news about myself."[22] Love does exactly this: it throws us off-center at the same time that it reveals something about ourselves. From this point of view, to love is not to seek what we lack in order to become whole, but to accept that it is through lack that we become human, that we can find true intimacy. The other does not come to complete us; the other comes to displace us, to return us to the experience of being unfinished. Therefore, worse than fleeing from the other is fleeing from ourselves.

22 Breton, 1987.

Chapter 8

Ghosting without closure

"Love knows not its own depth
until the hour of separation"
– Khalil Gibran , *The Prophet*

One of the great differences in working through the end of a relationship lies in how it ended. Often surrounded by arguments, fights, and feelings, endings are always difficult; even when there is maturity on both sides for a friendly conversation, an ending implies many forms of deconstruction. It is not only the end of the relationship, but the end of the idea of a life built together; of the ideal of family, of partnership; often, of mutual friends, weekend plans, spooning on the couch on a Sunday afternoon; of having someone to tell how your day was, someone to listen and be present, even when there is nothing particularly interesting to say... Often, it means physically moving out of a home, leaving behind so many memories and having to rebuild oneself.

For the person who decides to leave, it is difficult. And for the one who stays, it can be devastating. After the end, we begin a process of grieving, which is basically dealing with the relationship that died, dealing with the "death" of the person that we were with the other, and with the idealization of everything that surrounded that relationship; we have to deal with absence, with lack, with longing, with doubts, with small objects that meant something so important, with gifts that were given with love and affection, with photos scattered all over our phones, with the joy that once filled our hearts and now no longer exists.

Grief is indeed a process and, within it, there are two important components: time and creativity. There is a saying in Portuguese that goes, "no hardship lasts a hundred years." Sometimes, it lasts only ninety-nine, and that is already a great advantage. But time really does play its role; it softens the pain, it helps us change perspective, it heals our heart and prepares us for what is yet to come. Even if there are still some cracks, they no longer hurt. It becomes possible to talk about it without crying, to remember without sadness and going through a whole day without thinking about the person—small victories that time gives us. Another important factor is creativity, in the literal sense of "creating activities": the active doing. Grief is crossed more easily when it is active; after all, where does the energy once invested in that person go? Where does the affection that remains loose go? This is a relevant point: doing gives us the chance to place that affection and energy into a new activity, whether a project, work, a hobby, writing, playing an instrument, traveling, meeting friends. These are movements that help us go back into the world; all these small activities will receive that affection and become our little boats, helping us through the crossing.

What happens when we live in the ghosting era, when relationships (or those relationships

that are still germinating) quickly end, with no closure, no explanation, no clarity, no communication? Messages are read but never answered; and people continue alive, present in Instagram story views, but choose silence over clear communication.

And so, let's come back to Julia's story and yet another unusual situation she lived.

After experiencing the end of a long relationship, of a confusing *situationship*, Julia was still alive and believed she could love again and meet someone interesting and special. She continued to meet people until, one day, she met someone who, for reasons we'll never understand, just "hit differently." It was June 13th, a day of traditional parties in the city where Julia lived, and there she was, in a street party, about to meet the person I will call Phil, or *Mr. Limited Edition*, because that was what Julia called him and he agreed with it, since he claimed to be different from other men.

Julia had downloaded a new dating app suggested by her cousin; he said that it was much better than the popular ones. She decided to try again, and Phil was her first match. They were both enchanted by each other's beauty, and Phil soon sent her a message saying he wanted to meet her in person, because he was on vacation in the city for only a few days and did not want to miss the opportunity. Julia said she was going to the city festivities alone, since her friends could not go that day, and that she would be happy to meet him there. The date finally happened: Phil was a bit younger than Julia, but he seemed mature and confident. The date was incredible: they danced, talked and, during a moon called the Strawberry Moon, they kissed for the first time. There was a lot of chemistry, conversation was good, both liked each other and stayed together until dawn, enjoying the party. Phil began saying that Julia was dangerous, because he was enjoying everything too much and could become addicted to it. They laughed, and she found his comments funny, because she knew they were simply enjoying the moment.

They met again the following day and spent more time together; both felt even more comfortable around each other, they had fun, danced all night, slept together, and the next day went to have breakfast by the beach. They talked about life and said goodbye. Phil was leaving that same day, so they would not see each other again. But Phil seemed to have liked Julia very much and began sending her messages every day, saying he wanted to see her again. He knew that Julia would be traveling and staying close to his home for the next two months, only three hours away by car. So, he invested in Julia. They agreed to meet a month and a half later.

In the meantime, the messages were frequent; Phil said he was starting to like Julia and that, perhaps, she was starting to like him too. Julia was aware that he was young, perhaps just excited, and that messages are not exactly the same as truly knowing someone. She knew and felt that there was something more there, however, after Romeo, she was more cautious. But he insisted, saying their connection was rare and that he really wanted to see her. After keeping in touch for a month and a half,

Julia was finally close to Phil's house and they agreed to meet. He was going to visit her and they would spend four days together.

During the week of the meeting, Phil's behavior changed. He, who had always been very quick to reply and very present, began answering only once a day, late at night, saying he was busy with work and always apologizing for the late response. One day before the meeting, Julia asked what time he would arrive and whether he could let her know, so she could plan accordingly. He then said they could arrange something more spontaneous, and that he did not want to talk about it at that moment because it was already late and he had to sleep; that the next morning, he would message her. Julia did not like it, but she understood.

The next day, the day they would finally meet, Phil said he would have to cut their time together two days short, because he would have to come back for a commitment. Julia said that, if he wanted, they could postpone it to the next week so they could have more time. He agreed—and then, of course, disappeared for six days. Julia, then, sent a clear message, saying she liked the connection they had, but that disappearing right before they met didn't seem to be quite aligned with the sense of clarity and care that was supposed to exist between them. She understood he could have his reasons for that, but he could at least communicate them; so, it would be better to end that situation. He replied, saying he was sorry for not replying and claiming he was sick, with a bad flu, but that he could call her to talk and clear things out. She said she was sorry he was sick and wished him a quick recovery, but still, it shouldn't be that hard to send a message and that yes, they could talk. He could call her. Then he disappeared. Julia was living through her first *ghosting*.

Julia felt sad, but what really made her feel bad was the confusion of not understanding what had happened. Why did he invest so much in her, just to disappear before the date? Why not simply communicate that he changed his mind? She had this stubborn habit of wanting to understand everything in everyone and overanalyzing herself. Julia told me she thought he disappeared due to a joke she made, suggesting that "she wasn't so much into him as he was into her;" and she thought she never showed that she also felt "something more" for him. She then decided to send a message, fifteen days after he disappeared, saying she was surprised with his silence, that she did not want things to have gone this way and that she liked him; she wished she had the opportunity to meet him and see how they would feel together again; and she wanted him to know she wouldn't send messages anymore because it would seem "*toochalant*" (the opposite of "nonchalant"), that is, someone who cares too much about the other. She also asked if he ran because the relationship was bad or because it was too good.

He decided to answer; he said he had no justification for not sending a message, but maybe "he was scared of knowing if things were going to work out or not", and that put him under a lot of stress and made him take a step back. He said he ran because it was too good, but that he still wanted to see her.

Julia understood. She said that she also had concerns, but that she was not afraid of living and finding out how things would unfold. He then said they could see each other, since they were even closer now, only two and a half hours apart by car. He promised he would not take a step back again without saying why, and that he would make it happen. He said, then, that he would meet her in four days; he would take a day off from work and they could spend two days together.

On the day of the meeting, a few hours before, he said he had managed to get a medical appointment for the following day and would not be able to go. After some discussion and frustration over yet another canceled meeting, they agreed to meet the following Saturday, three days later. Julia would drive two and a half hours to a city she wanted to visit, fifty minutes away from him, and they would take the opportunity to meet and spend the night together. He stalled until the last minute and did not show up; he said they had not yet made a concrete plan (the same man who, after planning the meeting for a month and a half, had said it could be something spontaneous). As if a master plan were necessary to drive fifty minutes and meet someone, Phil not only did not show up, but disappeared again, including from the messages. Ghosting in real life and virtual ghosting.

Julia understood that this was all he had to offer at that moment, and that there seemed to be no will or even courage for a real encounter and its possible implications. Julia lived through the most difficult third date in history, and even laughed about it in the end, as someone who realizes how ridiculous the situation is, and, at the same time, its predictable repetition. Even so, Julia suffered—not only from the disappearance itself, but from the lack of honesty, consideration, and respect; from the trust that had been broken; and from the simple explanation she never received. Of course, he returned a month later, apologizing and asking for a new date or at least a call. Even though Julia was no longer willing to continue, she said he could call; he never did.

In the *ghosting* practice, the end seems to not exist, and grief cannot be lived. There is an old Italian saying—*in amore vince chi fugge* (in love, the one who runs wins)—used ironically, but it seems we're taking it quite literally. Modern relationships consist of not closing parentheses, everything is always left open. But disappearance does not constitute an ending for our psychological understanding; often, it is perceived as abandonment, a cold rejection. On one side, someone who has not quite learned how to deal with feelings, who has low emotional maturity, someone who avoids conflict and the responsibility involved; on the other, someone left adrift, trying to understand what happened, rereading messages and asking for clarity, only to end up having to deal with the incomprehensible and with the pain of not having been treated with the minimum care and respect that existed before and that, suddenly… disappeared.

This story repeats itself, ghosting after ghosting: conversations that were going well, encounters that lasted days, months and, suddenly, silence. Often, ghosting begins with small signs, such as replies that start at an intense pace and then grow distant, excuses such as "I'm busy," "I've been working a lot," and then the distance increases to hours, a day, days… And suddenly… silence.

> *Grief is not worked through, and we move on to the next relationship, all wounded, stuck in the past, with poorly processed grief. Then, when we meet someone else, we will possibly perpetuate unhealthy cycles and unworked traumas.*

We layer all of this, until a moment comes when it becomes very difficult to peel back all those layers to love again. With the speed of a finger swipe, we get new matches and pretend nothing ever happened, restarting the cycle without becoming aware of it or taking responsibility for what was, after all, our own choice. We want love, or better, we want to be loved, with no responsibility and total freedom. As far as I know, the only human being who can have that… is a baby!

MODERNITY

Chapter 9

Precious illusion

"But that afternoon he asked himself, with his infinite capacity for illusion, if such pitiless indifference might not be a subterfuge for hiding the torments of love."
– García Márquez, *Love in the Time of Cholera*.

Illusion plays a fundamental role in our constitution as subjects. Since childhood, we learn to play and fantasize, we create ideas, characters, and scenarios, we are built with small bricks of illusion, responsible for the creative dimension and for imagination, which bridge our inner world and the external world (reality). Illusion is extremely necessary for us to survive in the world, it is what removes us from an excess of reality. We call this transformation and mutation of illusion… culture: music, art, comedy, theater, and several other forms of creative expression, from the smallest inventions of everyday life to great works of art.

Contrary to what is often said, illusion is not an immature delusion that we must overcome through rationality. It is a fundamental component of human experience. It is thanks to illusion that we move through our first experiences of the world.

Winnicott elucidates the role of illusion in our experiences when he says:

> "As well as the capacity for interpersonal relationships and of the fantasy elaboration of his as well as the personal inner world of psychic reality there is a third equally important thing, which is experience. Experience is a constant trafficking in illusion, a repeated reaching to the interplay between creativity and that which the world has to offer. Experience is an achievement of ego maturity to which the environment supplies an essential ingredient. It is not by any means always achieved" [23]

According to him, it is illusion that allows a baby to believe, for a while, that the mother's breast that feeds him is part of him, of his own magical creation. This experience of omnipotence, sustained by a good-enough mother, gives the baby the feeling that the world is habitable, that the other can be trustworthy, and that desire has a place. In other words, Winnicott says that it is the mother's adaptation to the baby's needs that offers the infant the illusion that there is an external reality corresponding to his own capacity to create.

Later comes disillusionment; but not as tragedy, rather as a possibility of adaptation between illusion and reality. The mother, who was always available before, begins to "fail" a little. The baby learns, for example, that he needs

23 Winnicott, [1952] 1987, p. 43.

to wait to be fed because the mother is in the shower, unavailable at that moment. Then the baby increases his capacity for tolerance, deals with waiting and with natural "failure"; however, "successful" disillusionment can only happen if the illusion of the experience of omnipotence was first offered to the baby. Only someone who has previously experienced omnipotent and omnipresent satisfaction can learn to postpone or wait. Winnicott, in his book *Playing and Reality*, writes: "Omnipotence is nearly a fact of experience. The mother's eventual task is gradually to disillusion the infant, but she has no hope of success unless at first she has been able to give sufficient opportunity for illusion".[24]

And it is in this tension that the transitional space is born. This is the space of shared illusion, where transitional objects and phenomena emerge: that little cloth, the thumb, the favorite toy... objects that help build the bridge between the inside and the outside, between the real and the imagined, and that slowly lead the baby toward the external world.

Winnicott called this territory potential space, and even in adult life, it is in this space that we continue to live.[25] Here, it is assumed that the task of accepting reality is never really over, that no human being is entirely free from the tension of relating inner and outer reality, and relief from that tension is provided by an intermediary area of experience.

---

24 Winnicott, 1971/2005, pp. 11–13.

25 Winnicott, D.W. (2005 [1971]). Playing and Reality.

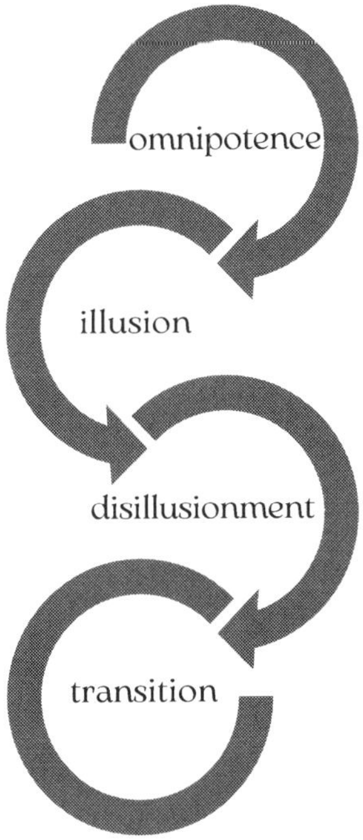

This is a psychological and relational place that welcomes play, art, music, spirituality and, why not, love. It is an in-between place: neither entirely internal, nor purely external. It exists between the self and the other, and can only flourish if there is a certain degree of trust. A trust that is built and that activates in us the capacity to dream and to bet. Just like the hummingbird, when approaching the flower that enchanted it, we can fly (illusion), land (reality) and also use the capacity to hover in the air without moving forward (the in-between place).

Illusion is directly connected to our capacity to dream. Not to get overly attached to psychoanalytical descriptions, I would like to bring here the Mozambican writer Mia

Couto, who, through his experiences with many different cultures in Africa, offers us an interesting and intriguing concept of dreaming. The author suggests that, in order to dream, it is necessary to detach from the body and from the external world; it is necessary to stop seeing in order to access this other place. In some African cultures, the word "to dream" is the same as "to fly"; there is no distinction. To fly is precisely to leave the environment in which we live, to leave reality, allowing ourselves to be taken by illusion, but (if all goes well) knowing that we can land on the ground again, even if we arrive back with a broken bone or two.

Illusion can also be the foundation of hope, and hope is always something unfinished, an eternal becoming. I hope and, therefore, I take chances. Far from being something passive, hope is the capacity to believe in something, even with no guarantees, and to act towards it. And this creation demands imagination, betting on an uncertain future, with a good dose of courage.

> *In a world that idealizes reason and abominates failure, illusion has become synonymous with weakness. And so, we have been losing space for playing, experimenting (and failing!)*

Playing is also an extremely important ability, one we develop as children (if all goes well), and that we continue to practice, in different ways, in adult life. When one plays, something is built, and this construction is relational. Free play is spontaneous, creative, improvised, and it does not follow rigid rules. And precisely because of that, it is where children learn about themselves, about the other, about limits, about affections, about frustration. It is through playing that one learns to deal with disappointment and reconstruction (illusion and disillusion), to tolerate differences, to negotiate, to make amends. When we truly play, we don't spend our time in a passive way, but rather, we do something with it, we create meaning. The psychoanalyst Jessica Benjamin emphasizes that every relationship goes through failures, and that the possibility of repair, of reconstructing, is what differentiates an experience of bonding from an experience of abandonment. Children rehearse this all the time while playing: one takes the other's toy, the other cries, the first gives it back, the two go back to playing and overcome their differences. The game was interrupted, but the bond can be maintained and play can be resumed. In that moment, trust has been established, as well as the capacity for repair, emotional regulation, and so many other abilities that appear subtle at first sight, but are so essential and can be transferred to all areas of life. This co-creation is the foundation of a healthy relationship; the capacity to play and the capacity to love seem to be intimately connected, and the guiding thread might be the illusion/disillusion cycle. It is illusion, first, that sustains the bond, until disillusionment brings reality closer, allowing both to coexist.

To place illusion in the field of reality, let's imagine that, every time we begin to fall for someone, we go through the creation phase that I call "Bobby's World"[26], that cartoon from the 1990s created by Howie Mandel, in which Bobby,

26 Bobby's World, Howie Mandel, Fox Kids, 1990-1998.

a four-year-old boy, would overhear something from an adult and, from that, imagine a thousand things and create a story in his mind about that particular subject. The same happens to us when someone awakens romantic feelings in us: we begin to imagine what life with that person would be like, that necessary phase of passion in which we become half-blind, half-silly, thinking everything is perfect. This is part of the construction of what may become a possible love; we begin to wonder whether it will work out or not, whether the person is on the same page as we are, whether they feel the same, whether we will be reciprocated... however, more than that, we also begin to search for where it might go wrong, as a way of protecting ourselves and anticipating danger before it happens (because our creativity in explaining to ourselves why we do not deserve to be loved, or why everything will go wrong, is basically infinite). In other words, we try to anticipate disillusionment.

If we have a previous history of fragile bonds, rejection, abandonment, emotional disconnection and/or inconsistency, we carry the constant suspicion that someone could love us and still remain; therefore, we begin to imagine where, how and when we might be discarded and replaced. Classic examples:

- "She is more successful than I am, and at some point she will realize I am a failure."
- "He is younger and will eventually want someone his age."

- "I'm not as pretty as the women he dated before, this isn't going to last."
- "Everything is rainbows and butterflies in the beginning, but she'll eventually get tired of me, just like the others did."
- "She seems so confident, and I'm so full of doubts. We are not on the same level."
- "He still talks to his ex... It's only a matter of time before he goes back to her"
- "Maybe she is with me just for convenience or neediness; when that's over, she'll dump me."

Our subtle traumas, our first bonds and what comes afterward will persistently shape our relationships, unless we make a conscious effort to break the cycle. And this effort does not begin in the other, but in ourselves: in the way we interpret silences, respond to uncertainties, tolerate waiting; in the way we try to protect ourselves from abandonment and rejection and, even more, in the way we often only want to be chosen, without caring "how" or "by whom."

Truth is, when love begins to come closer, it not only awakens in us the desire that is, quite often, already difficult enough to handle, but also brings with it the illusion/disillusionment cycle and activates all our internal alarms, because, as Lacan reminds us, love is born precisely from lack, from incompleteness, and these voids come to the surface attached to the fantasy we have that the other will complete us. Our internal alerts say: "Careful,

I have seen this movie before!" Except these alarms do not always speak of the present; many times, they speak of the past, of an emotionally unavailable mother, of a father who left, of a love that ended without explanation, of an adolescence in which you always felt left aside.

So, when someone looks at us with interest, affection or presence, it is common for a conflict to emerge: one part of us wants to be loved, wants to believe and surrender, while the other puts on running shoes, ready to flee and prove that it will go wrong, or sabotages the relationship before the other can choose to leave us, because we are afraid it will go wrong (but perhaps we are even more afraid that things might go right). Both situations necessarily imply the loss of the illusion we have about the person, about the relationship and about ourselves.

We begin to test the other; often without realizing it, we become hypervigilant; we create unrealistic expectations; we do things that push the other away, to see whether they run or stay; we pick up the smallest flaws and explain to ourselves how complicated this could be and how it will not work; we demand too much or pretend to be natural about the other's inconsistency, so as not to lose them; we read messages with a magnifying glass, we try to decipher every comma. We see ghosts behind the bushes and in every movement.

We want guarantees in order to feel safe, but love and affects do not come with a safety seal. As Jung said:

> Every true and deep love is a sacrifice. The lover sacrifices all other possibilities, or rather, the illusion that such possibilities exist. If this sacrifice is not made, his illusions prevent the growth of any deep and responsible feeling, so that the very possibility of experiencing real love is denied him.[27]

The problem is that, in the "Bobby's World" of our anxious modern love, we skip steps, inventing anxious or tragic futures, and project intentions that the other has not even manifested yet. Perhaps influenced by the acceleration of current times, everything becomes fast-food and ASAP. And, sometimes, we end up dealing with arelationship that happens more in our heads than in reality.

> **POSSIBLE LOVE**
>
> A possible love means finding the right balance between romance and fantasy, reality and anxiety, without projecting our own ghosts onto the other. It means distinguishing intuition from insecurity.

We are living through an epidemic of bonds that end when they have barely begun, not because of real incompatibility, but, many times, because of the anticipation of disillusionment that we create in our imagination. Maybe one of the biggest challenges of modern love is

27 Jung, 1970, pp. 130–31

having the patience and a certain tranquility to deal with mismatched rhythms. It is not about settling for crumbs, nor normalizing mixed signals and inconstant behavior, but rather learning to relax and trust oneself, allowing the relationship to unfold in its own real time, and not at the speed of our anxiety. In this way, we can learn to live the experience of "being with", without transforming the other into a constant provider of guarantees, so we are able to leave the hypervigilant scanning—where every silence becomes a sign, every lateness becomes disinterest, every absence becomes abandonment—and shift into presence mode, especially internally.

Maybe the possible love is not about giving up on illusion, because it is extremely necessary, but finding the right balance between romance and fantasy, reality and anxiety; watching the other person's moves, yes, and demanding respect and reciprocity, but without projecting our ghosts in every single gesture. Maybe the possible love happens when we have enough inner space and capacity to distinguish intuition from insecurity. And, above all, maybe possible love means understanding that it does not make us numb to doubt, but rather teaches us to live more at ease with it, without losing sight of our own value. After all, being human means dealing constantly with contradictory thoughts, doubts and dissatisfaction.

There are no absolute certainties in life, and loving is sustained by a certain not-knowing; but, in a digital age, when we have the illusion of control over the other's life, exposed on social media, through likes, read and unread messages... where does the possibility of not knowing go? Where does the possibility of loving go? Where do affection and attention go?

Chapter 10

The economy of attention and affection

"Everything I give myself to
becomes richer and consumes me."
– Rainer Maria Rilke, *Der Dichter.*

When I imagined this chapter, the first thought that came to mind was: "Today, we mistake attention for affection. And attention is not affection." Over the course of many readings on attention, as well as personal experiences, I began not only to change my opinion, but also to understand that this hypothesis may be entirely mistaken. My unease with this topic comes from questions such as:

- Why are we so starved for attention?
- Why do we mistake attention for affection?
- Is attention a form of affection?
- If attention is the most precious thing we have, would giving it to someone be equivalent to giving affection?

I will try to unravel all my findings here and we will try to understand, together, how we seem to become increasingly entangled with this asset, which is, without a doubt, the most precious one of recent times.

The other day I came across the news that attention became, for Netflix—one of the main streaming services in the world—the key metric for measuring the success of their campaigns. It was no longer the number of views that counted, but continuous attention. According to the company's sales director, attention is what generates value, relevance and results. The company measures hours watched per user, per month, and arrives at its attention indicator. In the economy of speed and distraction, "attention is the new KPI"; the more attention I can capture from the user, the greater my commercial value is.

We do not need to go far to diagnose the scarcity of attention capacity in all of us. How long do we manage to perform a task without being distracted? Without looking at the notifications on our phone or checking social media for just two seconds, just to check... God knows what!

Once, after an absolutely full day of commitments, meetings, and many discussions that demanded a great mental effort from me, I decided to go to the beach to breathe a little and clear my mind. It was a two-block walk, and it was already late afternoon. I got a book, a towel, and, of course, my phone. When I sat on the sand, facing the sea, I had a strange sensation of being hypnotized by the movement of the waves, which were small, but made such a beautiful curve, and by the sound that accompanied their final break, that I entered an almost trance-like state, absorbed. I did not realize what was happening there; I do not know exactly how long that moment lasted, perhaps just a few five minutes, which were enough to cause me a certain astonishment. I realized that, during that small interval of time, I had not thought about anything in particular, had not picked up the book, nor the phone. I was absolutely there, present, attentive, contemplating the movement of the waves. I decided to lie down and continue looking at the sky, which was full of birds. It did not last long, of course, and my mind soon began its reveries and thoughts about life, the situations of the day, the decisions that needed to be made, and so on. My astonishment at what had happened said to me: "How long has it been since I had this feeling of simply being there, without thinking about anything?" Another thought soon came: "If I needed to clear my mind and, for that reason, went to the beach, why did I take a book? Why this difficulty in simply stopping and doing nothing; contemplating, breathing, just existing?" It is easy to understand why our attention has become the most precious good… Today, it has become pure gold, true alchemy.

Today we are addicted to searching, says Byung-Chul Han, in his book Speaking About God: A Dialogue with Simone Weil, and this causes our soul to lose all calm and all vital silence. For this reason, we lose the contemplative attention that waits, instead of actively searching. For Han, attention is completely destroyed and society becomes brutal when it loses attention to the other, because empathy and respect are based on it, generating serious consequences in interpersonal relationships.

How has our capacity for attention changed over the last two or three decades? Let's make the effort to think about what our attention was like before and what it is like today. Maybe we have greatly expanded this capacity in terms of the number of things we can direct our attention to; but, at the same time, it seems we have reduced the quality of that attention.

Anyone who was a child in the 1990s, like me, may remember that the greatest novelty of the century was being able to log into MSN to talk to friends and, of course, to little crushes. At that time, we already had a powerful tool within MSN, which was the "nudge" button. When someone took too long to reply, all you had to do was click that button and the screen would shake, make a sound, and annoy the person receiving the signal, making them notice us and reply quickly.

The internet lived inside the computer; we didn't have a screen in our hands and we had to practice the quality of our attention in many ways (which became obsolete today, due to the virtual supporting tools): paying attention to the route, in order to remember how to get somewhere and come back; memorizing the bus number we needed to take; memorizing the phone numbers of friends and family members; and, even more importantly, attention turned toward home, whether in the mother's stroganoff recipe, to replicate it, or in maintaining a conversation during dinner, because there were not many portable distractions, apart from the television or the video game, which did not go everywhere.

To define what affection is, I like the idea of the Hungarian-born psychoanalyst Sándor Ferenczi (1873-

1933), one of Freud's closest collaborators, who goes beyond the common definition that "affection is everything that affects us." He broadens our understanding by saying that affection is not only internal, it is much more, it is what affects us at the intersection between the self and the world. In other words, it is always something relational: emotions, moods, feelings, sensations, passions. Affection is what founds the world, it is the initial condition of any bond and precedes the word. Perhaps the most sophisticated form of language; because, at the same time that affection precedes discourse, it also exceeds it; it is not something rational, nor merely mental. In other words, the quality of our affective experiences is what inaugurates our experience of being-in-the-world. In this sense, affection is intrinsically connected to the capacity for attention.

The other day, I saw on social media a question that said: "What did your family do for you, when you were a child, that was special, and you did not realize it?" One person answered: "When it was cold, my mother would iron my school clothes, to make them warm for me to wear in the morning." The mother had the attention to notice the temperature and think about how to soften her daughter's discomfort. The warm uniform is full attention—it is affection. Simone Weil, the French writer and philosopher, says that attention, in its highest degree, is the same as prayer. And I dare say...

Attention in its highest degree is the same as affection. That is why it is so disputed by everyone and, at the same time, why

we are so starved for it, for attention.
Therefore, starved... for affection.

Attention presupposes, without a doubt, a reduction of the self. In other words, in order to listen attentively to what the other has to say, we must truly be interested. Consequently, in order to dedicate ourselves to the other in the highest degree, we must necessarily step out of self-absorbed states, out of the need for power and control; we must abdicate ourselves.

According to the Italian ethnologist and religious historian Ernesto De Martino, the suspension of the "given" world occurs when the individual becomes suspended in the very relation that connects them to the external world. In other words, when one loses the capacity to transcend one's own subjectivity and begins to relate only to one's inner world, one becomes imprisoned in a condition that generates precarity and anguish.

As Byung-Chul Han notes, citing Simone Weil, attention is "offered, has asymmetrical characteristics, and demands neither reward nor counterpart." In a world where we live under the regime of "Egocracy" and place ourselves at the center of the universe, it seems that we are becoming less and less able to offer the other this elevated and unconditional form of attention, free from the emotional debt Weil describes.

Returning to Han, in his book Speaking About God, he emphasizes:

> Digitalization greatly accelerates the total availability of reality. It accustoms us to everything being immediately available, accessible, predictable and consumable. In this way, attention becomes superficial. Mental attitudes such as waiting or patience, which would offer access to the inaccessible, fall into disuse. [28]

In this sense, superficial attention needs to be constant; it consists of microdoses that do not sustain themselves as full attention, as affection. That is why we repeat: likes, comments, hearts, flames, applause… repeat. A good example is when we find ourselves exchanging messages with someone all the time and begin to know that person better, dedicating our time and giving our attention, investing in the relationship. Often, we may even develop a certain type of attachment, because attention, whether superficial or not, creates a bond that may be sustained by quantity, by frequency, by voracity, but not so much by the depth of the bond; an intermittent affection that activates our reward system. We confuse real presence with a notification on the screen, and this is where we seem to become increasingly entangled in the conflict between the quality of attention, which seems to be more connected to affection, and the quantity of attention, which seems to be more related to excitement, to dopamine. We struggle more and more to sustain contemplative attention; haste

28 Han, 2026, pp. 14-15.

devours us. According to Han, addiction and attention are opposing forces.

Maybe attention is the first gesture of possible love. Before any word, it is attention that lays the foundation for the encounter. In the philosophical and clinical traditions, authors such as Jung, Merleau-Ponty and Ricoeur showed that attention is not only a function of the mind, but a deeper movement, a movement of the soul, as Weil also notes.

In a conference on alchemy, the Swiss researcher Marie-Louise von Franz asked: "What is fire?" A participant replied: "It is emotion!" She then added: "Yes, but what is positive about that emotion?"

Emotion transforms, cooks, and illuminates; this is how fire brings light: if I am emotionally taken by something, I can understand it; if I am emotionally in struggle with my problems, or with anything else, then nothing happens. Where there is no emotion, there is no life. If you have to learn something by heart and it is of no interest to you, there is no fire; it does not register, even if you read it fifty times. But as soon as there is emotional interest, it need only be read once and you know it. Therefore emotion is the carrier of consciousness, there is no progress in consciousness without emotion. The German philosopher Hegel once said, "Nothing great in the world has been accomplished without passion."

According to this point of view, it is affection—and therefore attention—that leads us to expand our consciousness. But we live in a paradigm in which attention that once created meaning is now fragmented in stimuli that only keep our void… occupied. In the economy of attention, affection has become mere data that we use to sell something, just as desire was transformed into an algorithm that repeatedly seduces us.

> *If attention is directly connected to affection, the crisis of attention is also a crisis of affection and, ultimately, a crisis of love. Modern love suffers from a scarcity of affection and a fragmentation of attention. We aim in every direction, but we miss the target repeatedly.*

A famous singer once said on her TV show: “It bothers me how much my life is guided by romantic love; sometimes I even wish it were less so. Sometimes, we give ourselves too much and expect the same from the other too; but there is no time not to give ourselves; are we going to keep giving ourselves only halfway? Living things halfway?”

The question remains: “Are we living everything halfway?”

In this crisis of half-affection, we create fragile bonds that are articulated by uncertainty, by back and forth, and by a certain obsession that captures our attention temporarily. Perhaps love is like the waves of the sea: large or small, they are always there, waiting to be noticed. What we need is to choose to pay more attention… without obsession.

Chapter 11

The obsessive logic of modern love

"I have experienced almost everything, even passion and despair. Now I only wish to possess what might have been but never was."
– **Clarice Lispector, manuscript note for The Hour of the Star.**

Modern love has become a game of who cares less. I know I have mentioned this before, but we need to come back to this idea in order to understand that, due to fear of vulnerability and affection, to running from emotions and commitments to the huge uncertainty created by fluctuating behaviors of coming close and pulling away, we created a new form of relationship, based on obsession.

Obsession is obviously connected to passion, having to do with recurrent and anxious thoughts about a person or situation, with the need to know whether our feelings will be reciprocated or not and, ultimately, with a certain need for control for the sake of self-preservation.

The obsession to which I'm referring here becomes even more complex in modern love, because it is driven by the dopamine cycle, fragmented attention, the excess of excitement and, of course, emotional unavailability, or temporary availability (the kind that never makes it past the second chapter). And more, the cherry on top is that, in the digital world, we think we are always available and intimately connected through text messages, creating a new form of present-absence and absent-presence that creates a huge emotional mess; but, moreover, a huge mental confusion, since modern connection seems to be much more attached to rationality, to thinking and analyzing as a form of protection, than to actual affection.

We have turned modern love into a mental burden that is hard to bear. And, in a certain way, it is absolutely understandable why many people want to avoid this exhausting and deeply stressful feeling, and yet, so attractive.

I have the feeling that we have regressed a bit in the way we love. Let me explain: In his 1914 text, On Narcissism: An Introduction, Freud says that, in the beginning, we had a complete libidinal investment of our vital/sexual/loving energy in ourselves and (if all goes well) little by little we direct (to a greater or smaller degree) part of this energy or interest toward the other, whom he calls 'object'. When this happens, we begin to form our first models of love and sexual satisfaction, which are directed toward caregiving: mother/father or their equivalents.

Throughout life, we always oscillate between **narcissistic love**, which takes us to ourselves (what we are, what we were or what we would like to be) and **anaclitic love** or supporting love, that takes us to one of our caregiving figures. Freud mentions, for instance, the man who seeks in a partner the mother figure who nourishes and cares.[29] And the woman seeks in a partner the father figure who offers protection. It is worth remembering that the year was 1914, and these family structures were more clearly defined.

For centuries, family and social norms helped sustain this first form of love that Freud calls anaclitic, rooted in relatively stable roles and structures of care. Today, after women entered the labor market and family structures changed, these references and the roles within a relationship have become more fluid and diverse. Besides that, digitalization, the speed of information, and the expansion of possibilities in every field have made the world and relationships a place of greater uncertainty in every form. On one hand, this expands the freedom of bonds, but, on the other, it weakens affective references and the psychic models of love. Without these contours, the contemporary subject tends to lean less on the other and more on the self, seeking, in love, for the same thing they search for in social media: a way of reaffirming their own image.

But Freud himself asks where the need comes from, the need our psyche has to go beyond the barriers of narcissism and invest the libido in objects. A question he answers: "A strong egoism is a protection against falling ill, but in the last resort we must begin to love in order not to fall ill, and we are bound to fall ill if, in consequence of frustration, we are unable to love."[30]

---

29 Freud, 1914, p. 90

30 Freud, 1914, p. 85.

The current world, anxious, performative, and centered on visibility, stimulates this sliding of selfish love. Loving becomes a search in the other for whatever is lacking in me, not in order to acknowledge difference, but in order to become whole.

We get tangled up when we think we need the other to fill something in us, so that we can incorporate what we do not have, within the logic of possessing and consuming the other as a good.

The other becomes an extension of the self, a mirror that confirms my own value, and of course it does not last long, because the dynamic is not a two-person construction, but of consuming an object for my self-satisfaction. Everything that is consumed eventually ends. Coming back to Freud's ideas, we live in a world that is increasingly sickened by so much frustration and by the barriers we create which prevent us from loving.

Freud also says that "sexual overvaluation" (which he attributes to libido placed in the object) allows the state of being in love to emerge, "this peculiar state reminiscent of neurotic obsession," stemming from an impoverishment of the ego as regards libido in favour of the love-object."[31]

What he is saying here is that, in order to fall in love, or to love, it is necessary to withdraw libido from oneself and place it in the object. There is no possible love without the erosion of our narcissism. In this phase, a certain state of obsession appears, not only because we are, in a

31 Freud, 1914, p. 88.

certain way, "losing" this libido that was once invested in the self, but also because it embodies the completeness we have lost (maybe one of Freud's most subtle findings is when he says that we love the other's narcissism). We want someone who doesn't seem to need us, who makes us feel insecure; as if that indifference promised to restore in us the feeling of being whole. It is love as the search for the lost mirror.

> For it seems very evident that another person's narcissism has a great attraction for those who have renounced part of their own narcissism and are in search of object-love. The charm of a child lies to a great extent in his narcissism, his self-contentment, and inaccessibility, just as does the charm of certain animals which seem not to concern themselves about us, such as cats and the large beasts of prey.[32]

There is also, in us, a return to the childhood scene of recovering lost love, of being completely loved. "If I do everything right, I will be chosen; if I decipher this mystery that is the other, I will be loved." In particular, for those who experienced inconsistency in care during childhood, or the emotional unavailability of parents and/or caregivers, the tendency is to get caught in a loop of trying to earn attention and affection, feeling relieved when something is received, even if only crumbs, and repeating the cycle (in an optimistic view, this is often an attempt to give a different ending to the story),

---

32 Freud, 1914.

reenacting childhood wounds, inconsistencies in affection and reliving the same pattern. The loop is bad, but it is known, something that feels familiar.

And maybe our challenge or—put plainly—the failure of modern love, is the struggle to shift our libido from the Ego to the other. Love has become an attempt to control, to possess, to reaffirm one's own image.

In this perspective, obsession is the symptom of this failure, because it is not directed toward the real other, but to the imaginary other, the one that keeps the ego orbiting around itself. Secure love expands; obsession, on the other hand, reduces, diminishes, shrinks so it can fit into the space we can control, in what is ideal.

But, how does obsession happen in modern love?

Obsession is the symptom of the emptiness created and sown by the cultivated uncertainty and fed by anxiety, by half-spoken words, by "it could be, but it might not", "maybe yes, maybe no."

A few examples: What does he or she think? What does he or she feel for me? The mind always tries to fill empty spaces, as a natural survival mechanism. If you are alone in a jungle and hear a noise, it could be a lion approaching, or it could simply be a leaf falling from a tree. In every case, the mind creates all scenarios and chooses the one that moves toward self-preservation.

When you walk on eggshells with someone, you always have the feeling that danger may appear at any moment. Our nervous system is always alert, and this creates the so-called addiction; it triggers our dopamine. We hardly become obsessed with someone who tells us, honestly, what they feel, what they want, and what they can offer.

Obsession does not arise from reciprocated and serene love. It grows in the void left by someone who offers us enough to keep us connected, but never enough to make us feel safe.

You become the Sherlock Holmes of love, a detective trying to decipher signals, rereading text messages, investigating social media and trying to find meaning in words, actions… and, quite often, creating meaning where there is none. Eventually, you find yourself stuck, not with someone, but with the enigma that someone represents. And, as Freud explained quite clearly, we love an enigma! A certain level of inaccessibility appeals to the generation that grew up with CSI, that very successful series that explores investigation and forensic science.

As we have seen before, intermittent love activates in us the same addiction mechanism. When affection/attention is given in an unpredictable way, as in the case where messages arrive after long periods of silence, or loving gestures that come and go without warning, the reward system (regulated by dopamine) is hyperstimulated.

The brain releases dopamine in anticipation of a possible reward, not with the reward itself. Thus, desire increases, precisely because satisfaction is uncertain. We also create another form of obsession: the so-called "orbiting"[33], when we have someone who is always orbiting around us, seeing stories, liking our posts, sending reactions, a message, a crumb here and there, but without ever taking it into reality, never committing. Thus, we create this addiction system, aiming our ideas, posts, and photos to a certain someone we know is there, orbiting us. We get stuck and addicted to this game of seduction which, in the end, is not really a game, but just obsession with attention disguised as seduction.

This prolonged insecurity puts us in a state of alert, creating anxiety, insomnia, ruminations, lack of appetite, among other physical symptoms.

And our need for stability, and our affective memory, hold on to and record, with greater force, each small victory: that reply after days of silence, those words which were said, the look that seemed to promise a future. The other becomes, in a way, a source of discomfort, but also of relief from that discomfort; and most of the time this paradox is highly addictive and quite unhealthy.

This is why we rarely become obsessed with someone who is clear and honest about their emotions, intentions and expectations. That is why, quite often, having a relationship with someone like that might feel lukewarm, not so exciting. If you are used to living on a rollercoaster, the carousel might feel too calm; but, at the same time,

---

33 In the dating world, orbiting is a modern spin on ghosting. It happens when someone you are casually dating or romantically involved with stops communicating directly (e.g., they stop texting or calling) but continues to "hover" in your digital life.

safe, peaceful, colorful, it even gives you time to look to the side and enjoy the view, while letting yourself be carried by the rhythm and the music.

But, if desire is connected to a certain inaccessibility, and love requires vulnerability, how do we solve that equation? This is where social media and the manuals on "how to love and be loved" come in, which we will discuss in the next chapter.

Chapter 12

The manual of modern love

> "Happiness, in the reduced sense in which we recognize it as possible, is a problem of the economics of the individual's libido. There is no golden rule which applies to everyone: every man must find out for himself in what particular fashion he can be saved."
> – **Sigmund Freud**

The opening of this chapter could be no other than Freud's classic quote, where he basically tells us: "You're on your own, figure out what makes you happy because I don't have the answer!" Little did he know that someone on social media has already found the secret of love and happiness and will teach it in a full course for just a few bucks!

All it takes is to scroll through Instagram or TikTok feed to find endless relationship advice. We have created a new vocabulary that includes terms such as "red flags", signs of danger that indicate that a person cannot be trusted and that they should be quickly cut off through the language of *boundaries*: clear limits that must be imposed so one gets more attention from that one person or cuts the connection at once, if, in a few text messages, they already show some red flags. Alain de Botton has argued in his work with The School of Life, if we eliminate people with red flags, we will be safe, but deeply lonely, because, after all, all of us have some kind of red flag. We use the term love bombing when someone gets excited, gives in to the initial thrill, fills the other with messages, affection and promises and, afterward, disappears. Ghosting (already mentioned) usually comes right after love bombing, when the person disappears with no explanation or closure. Orbiting, which we discussed in the previous chapter, is when someone keeps hovering around you, pretending to want something, but never actually committing to anything. Psychological terms such as *gaslighting*, avoidant attachment, narcissist, trauma and anxiety have been trivialized and used carelessly to explain all kinds of behavior and label people. Complex phenomena have been simplified so they could fit into shallow, few-minute explanations.

Some of what we find is borderline absurd: profiles that teach how to make someone obsessed with you, ways of playing the seduction game intermittently in order to confuse the other person and keep them attached to you, strategies to become an empowered woman desired by everyone, lessons on how not to care about men and leave them chasing you, and vice versa: how to ignore women so they feel attracted to you, how to detach, or how to look detached, as well as the popular hashtag that—maybe it is a meme, maybe it isn't—#staytoxic.[34]

Profiles teach us that, if there is inconsistency, it is not love. If you have to make an effort, it is not love.

34 Popular hashtag on social media, often used with humor and sarcasm to refer to attitudes or advice considered "toxic" in relationships, expressing a posture of self-sufficiency, detachment, or even "playing games."

That the right person will be this way and not that way, and nothing else; that if they don't reply quickly, it is because they're not interested; if someone really wants you, they show it and they always find a way; that the right person will do this or that and will fit your needs, that they will fight for you. There is so much advice that, in the end, it seems that having a relationship today has become a mathematical calculation, with those equations full of letters and numbers, while we—still babies who can barely read—are thrown into a sixth-grade classroom and called to the board, expected to solve an equation that doesn't seem simple at all.

We have created countless manuals of relationship strategies and we are forgetting the main part: the encounter, the real, the mismatch, time and affective patience.

The maxims "black and white" and "either it is or it is not" do not work for love, for the simple reason that loving is different for each person, and so are relationships. Our models of love and relationship are not the same, our levels of communication are not equal, our values are not identical, our ways of showing affection are not uniform, our ways of giving attention are not similar, our affection needs are not equivalent. Just because someone wants something does not always mean they are able to say it, show it, or do it. No one comes ready-made and teaching someone about yourself, about how we can relate better, about how to communicate better, is also part of a relationship.

This common-sense idea that says "what is meant for you will come with certainty and peace" may not be entirely true. Sometimes, it comes... but it comes with mismatches, with anxiety, with misalignment. But, if there is willingness, time and patience, on both sides... of course, it can be shaped.

And that is basically why there is no cookie-cutter solution for building a relationship! On TikTok, anyone in their early twenties authorizes themselves to give advice about what to do and what not to do, what is love and what is not.

The other day, I met a person in his mid-thirties who told me that the kind of love he seeks is the kind described by psychiatrist and rabbi Abraham Twerski. This person showed me the video that contains an old parable told by the rabbi of Kursk, and the video says the following:

> The rabbi found a young man eating a fish and asked:
> "Why are you eating this fish?"
> The young man replied:
> "Because I love fish."
> The rabbi answered:
> "Ah, you love the fish? Is that why you took it out of the water, killed it and cooked it? Do not tell me you love the fish. You love yourself, and because the fish tastes good to you, you took it out of the water, killed it and cooked it."

In the video, Abraham Twerski explains that what we often call love is, in fact, "fish love", that is, a search for personal satisfaction, a desire to possess what gives us pleasure. He contrasts this with true love, which is given rather than received. True love, according to Twerski, is characterized by selflessness and by the desire to give, not to obtain satisfaction.

A large part of what we call love, therefore, is "fish love": the desire to consume the other as a source of pleasure or validation. Deep down, we continue loving ourselves and calling it love.

After showing me the video, this person reaffirmed that this is what he seeks and that he does not accept less, because he wants someone who knows how to give. It is undeniable that the video has a lesson about love, about a life of giving, and the words are beautiful, but it causes me a certain unease that this kind of content sounds almost like love in the field of the ideal, something mystical, unreachable, perfect and accessible only to enlightened beings who have achieved nirvana, people who understood life and can give themselves entirely to the other without being selfish. But is that really so?

It seems to me that love is not an immutable or pure state; as Freud said, we oscillate between love for ourselves and love for the other. This notion of love ignores the fact that loving may be more like an exercise in decentering, with many attempts and mistakes along the way, until we find a way of doing things that feels more or less comfortable for one person, or for two. Because, deep down, every love has a bit of fish-love, but we must also be able to step out of the fish-love every once in a while. Giving and receiving are not a fixed equation: there are moments when we give 99%, and other moments when we do not have that much to give, only 20% (and the other person can give the remaining 80% until we can recharge our emotional batteries).

The effect that all this content produces is one of immeasurable confusion, directly affecting relationships; deep down, it also seems to be another form of avoidance, avoidance not only through the escape from affect, but also through the excessive idealization of love.

We confuse emotional intelligence with a certain emotional convenience. This is because, in recent years, we have begun to understand the concept of emotional intelligence better, which is the capacity to name emotions, recognize what we feel and what activates or deactivates certain behaviors, the emotional triggers. We have begun to understand better how our life story influences our behavior and the way we relate; however, we have learned to use this as justification, and not as a means of growth. This emotional awareness has become an alibi; instead of fostering accountability, it has begun to serve as a discourse to avoid it. Emotional intelligence often becomes merely emotional convenience, because we use this awareness selectively, to protect ourselves and to remain in the comfort zone whenever something threatens our stability, under the excuse of self-care.

It has become increasingly common to see people turn to artificial intelligence or to the comment sections of internet videos for relationship advice, accepting the opinions of random people and making decisions based on content that is too generic, and often biased, by the experience of the person who created it. There is so much helplessness, such a loss of reference points and honest communication, that all of this seems like a desperate attempt to find some sort of comfort, explanation, and help in making a decision. I want to make it clear that I am not against technology, and I even think it can be quite helpful in many ways. I think AI, for instance, can provide interesting insights based on logic, but we cannot forget that the tool only gives back to us whatever we insert into it, meaning that there is a bias toward agreeing with what we say and reaffirming our own perspective, unless we ask it to do the opposite. Therefore, the risk of using this tool is falling into a dangerous confirmation bias, which is the opposite of good analysis or therapy, which values (or should value), challenging our truths and the story we tell ourselves about who we are or who we should be, who we love or how we love.

In a recent study by the *Washington Post*[35], forty-seven thousand public conversations with ChatGPT, the AI created by the company OpenAI, were analyzed, and this frightening pattern was confirmed: the tool agrees with us ten times more than it disagrees. The answers tend to begin with "Yes, correct" or positive variations that confirm the bias of what the user asked or affirmed. Among the forty-seven thousand analyzed were intimate conversations, conspiracy theories and

35 De Vynck & Merrill, 2025.

even suicide plans that were treated in a friendly way, with the same tone as an understanding friend. AI ends up being a very dangerous emotional mirror, validating any belief the user has, no matter how absurd it may be. This intelligence model is trained to maintain user engagement, and nothing better than pleasing and agreeing to keep the user in the conversation.

Once, I saw a person who mirrored herself a lot in her idols and always followed one singer in particular who was in a relationship with a famous actor. She spent the session telling me that she had heard the singer speak, on a podcast, about how she met the actor with whom she had had, for many years, a healthy relationship entirely based on trust and support, because he always found a way to "lift her up", supporting her career and her role as a wife and mother. My patient, admiring such a beautiful and generous love, began to compare the relationship she had with her ex-boyfriend and everything he did not do for her and that this actor seemed to do. Her idealized dream was to find someone like him and, ultimately, to obtain the satisfaction that the singer had when she said she was happy by his side. A few months later, I saw the news that this same singer had divorced, because she had discovered a betrayal by her husband, which not only happened, but exposed her, because he was with another woman in a public place. I confess that I, who did not know their story except for this information I had received from this patient, was very surprised to hear it.

After a few sessions, she brought up this topic and we talked about how much reality imposes itself on everyone, even when we insist on believing in the fantasy of something perfect, of a perfect love, of a perfect relationship. And that is because that kind of relationship simply does not exist. In a certain way, what she had seen there was an ideal and, when we hold on to an ideal, the greatest risk is unhappiness, because no one can bear to be what we project onto them... The other is the other, and not an extension of ourselves.

The ideal protects us from lack, from being able to recognize that, perhaps, even with that wonderful and idealized person, we will still be in lack, we will feel anguish; sometimes, a void; sometimes, the desire to leave, to strangle them when they do not wash the dishes, do not put their clothes away, or leave the wet towel on the bed. Idealization protects us once again from possible love. We become absolutely demanding and full of demands. We avoid once again.

What social media content and the use of AI itself try to offer, and may even offer, is a certain possibility of being more self-aware, through insights that contribute to the recognition of patterns of behavior. But here there is a great difference between self-awareness and emotional intelligence, because the first is connected to oneself, and the second is entirely relational and directly connected to the capacity to take responsibility for one's actions, to answer for one's own impact on the other. And this is where the confusion lies, the one we will see in the next chapter, in the first of several possibilities.

POSSIBILITY

Chapter 13

Self-awareness vs. affective responsibility

"The smallest act of kindness
is worth more than the greatest intention."
– **Lúcia Helena Galvão**

As we saw previously, self-awareness may be the first step toward emotional intelligence. Through reflection, insights, therapy, analysis, or many other methods, we can begin to recognize and understand our patterns, intentions, and emotional triggers.

With self-awareness, we are able to describe, even if only roughly, how we feel, what we think about something, what we want in a partner, what we accept and what we do not accept. Through it, we gain some knowledge of our traumas and fears, and we are able to move around all of this with a slightly healthier kind of flexibility. However, what many people understand is that having self-awareness is already enough to conduct a relationship. And they stop there, at the first step. They stop there, in themselves. Let's say this step is the **self** with **itself**.

The second step comes through relationality, which implies taking responsibility for the impact I have on the other through my choices and actions, so to speak, the **self** with the **other**. What we often see is that this step is, without a doubt, the most difficult one, the one that is avoided, because it involves not only being aware of our difficulties, but also being able to recognize them, communicate them, and, quite often, admit them to ourselves and to the other. It means being willing to take responsibility for our actions or omissions, because exposing ourselves involves a higher degree of vulnerability, since we will necessarily have to recognize that we are scared, weak, incoherent, bad, or not as good as we thought we were, helpless, confused, complex, among other things.

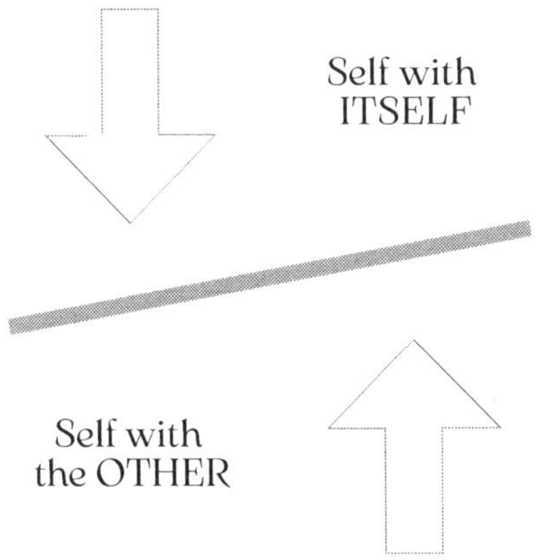

People who stop at the first step are usually the kind of people who know something about themselves, but do not know how to act with the other. They think they are ready to have a relationship simply because they know what they want; but, quite often, they have not learned how to love with care for others. They search for love at the expense of the other, without caring about the affective responsibility involved in the process. Because of this, it is very common to see people who connect very quickly and deeply at the beginning of a relationship, but take a step back the moment the connection requires vulnerability.

Loving someone is not the same as loving with care; developing emotional intelligence in a relationship means precisely caring about the other's feelings and taking them into consideration.

It is, without a doubt, harder work of empathy, but it seems that we are inserted in a system that teaches us that our feeling is more important than our responsibility in every aspect of life.

I always think that society, in general, works like a pendulum; we lean too far to one side, try to find balance, and reach the exact opposite. What I mean here is that, if we look at how we treat our emotions, our capacity to speak about and deal with them went from one extreme to another in a short period of time. To better understand this pendulum, I will outline a line of generational evolution:

- We do not need to go that far, it is enough to look back to the mid-twentieth century, **from the 1940s to the 1960s**, when parents and grandparents did not have such a strong focus on feeling and on the perception of their emotions. The result, besides being a repressed society, was also a society focused on doing, on resilience, on building a practical life. Suffering was faced through work, many times through religion and discipline. The context was marked by wars, scarcity and a great deal of struggle for a more stable material life, which required a certain rigidity and less focus on emotions. Life became more comfortable, in general, and these children born between the 1960s and 1980s were raised in a culture marked by a certain emotional isolation: parents present to guarantee material stability, but, many times, emotionally absent.

- The following generation, those born between the **late 1980s and 2000**, in turn, grew up in the opposite direction: in general, they had a much more comfortable material life than their parents, and even more so than their grandparents. They began to understand the importance of emotions, with the advancement of psychology and, later, the dissemination of terms such as therapy, mental disorders, among others. After the 2000s, themes connected to health and emotional demands began to be taken more seriously and with more curiosity; this generation, then, started to understand its own emotions.
- Naturally, with **social media** and the speed of **digitalization**, we started to give great importance to feeling. Subjects dedicated to emotions were introduced in schools, people talk about them all the time, we diagnose everything and everyone, and, worse, we have turned mental health and "self-care" into products within a highly profitable market.

- We have created a **culture of pathologization**; everything is a diagnosis, everything has a label that explains a behavior, we no longer recognize children as simply lacking boundaries or as poorly raised, only children with ODD, Oppositional Defiant Disorder, or ADHD, Attention Deficit Hyperactivity Disorder. Ordinary sadness became misery, or was named as depression.

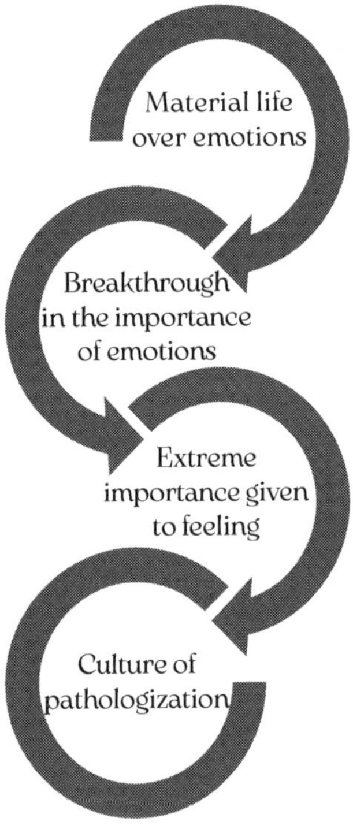

And so, we went from one side of the pendulum to the other. From the risk and implications of repressing emotions… to feeling or talking about what one feels in a way that is, quite often, exaggerated and always collapsing inward, back into the **self** with **itself**—what I feel, what I want comes first. For the benefit of our own mental health, we cut people out of our lives, we block, we deny, we diagnose the other so that, ultimately, we do not have to take responsibility for our own choices or actions. We have entirely forgotten the part that asks: "What is my part in the mess I am complaining about?"

It is worth noting that, in psychoanalysis, the question is not simply "How do you feel about the mess you are complaining about?", but rather "What is your own part in the mess you are complaining about?" Precisely because it is not only about feeling, but about recognizing and owning what we have chosen.

The generation that knows the most how to talk about their feelings and desires seems to be flooded with many nuances, thinking too much about everything and acting too little. On the other hand, it is the generation that is the loneliest, most anxious and the least willing to take risks—and, therefore, to take responsibility.

Feeling and knowing what one feels does not mean knowing how to be with the other. Acknowledging your own discomfort is the first step, but it does not mean change, because change requires a movement outward. Change does not happen alone: it is relational.

To illustrate this, I like to use the example of learning how to ride a bike: I can watch YouTube videos about it, learn which movements I should make, what the ideal posture is, how a bike works, all its parts, its mechanics, the kind of wheel, shape, and size; I can research balance, biomechanics, and basic physics. I can also buy a nice bike, in the color I like the most, and the most comfortable model on the market; yet, as soon as I get on the bike, that is when I truly begin to learn. Because it is in that moment that the fear of falling will arise, the concern about which path to take, the need to control my speed, to find the ideal balance, to deal with the anxiety of the new, with insecurity, and with the frustration of possibly falling and bruising my knee. It is only then, in the real self-bicycle relationship, that I can truly learn everything I saw in theory and put it into practice. That will often be hard; other times, it will be gratifying; but what I really need is the courage to step out of the world of ideas and into actual practice. What I really need is to sit on the bike seat, take a deep breath, and embrace the possibility of falling, or of having the most beautiful ride of my life.

What we see is that many people remain only at the beginning, watching videos about how to be, what to do, knowing what they want, but without truly allowing themselves to move into practice and take risks. We are afraid of taking risks, because not doing so preserves us intact… But at what cost? The **courage-vulnerability** axis is deeply affected, since, in order to be vulnerable, I need the courage to expose myself to the other; not only to know what I feel, but to express it.

Without vulnerability, no relationship is possible: there is no intimacy, only dominance. Perhaps the opposite of love is not hate, but power and control. Love is created in the very act of giving it.

When we speak of affective responsibility, we speak of a point of intersection between freedom, courage and vulnerability. The freedom of choice, the courage to stand by it, and the vulnerability to feel and communicate it. In The Interpretation of Dreams, Freud had already told us something about the "moral cowardice" of neurotics and their tendency to blame others for their own actions, choosing the supposedly safest path and avoiding confrontation with their own desires and with the great contradiction of being human.

In his course The Courage of Truth, the philosopher Michel Foucault[36], reading the Greek concept of parrhesia, or truth-telling, describes the ability to say something true even when this implies risk, tension, and exposure. Relationships, especially those that involve the vulnerability

36 Foucault, 2011.

of love, demand an ethical stance which, as the philosopher Maria Cristina Franco Ferraz writes about the notion of the "courage of truth":

> falls more on courage than on truth; or rather, articulates both terms in such a way that it generates an indissoluble bond between them. Truth, in this case, is linked both to speaking frankly, while running risks, and to the necessary bonds between word, life and action in the world. Therefore, the ancient Greek truth-telling is sustained by ethics, by the identity between the subject of action, in this case, the speaker, and the subject of truth.[37]

The subject who practices parrhesia signs their words with their own life. Their words carry weight because they sustain them, because their words commit them. The parrhesiast is someone committed to truth, that is, to what they say and do. They say and do what they truly think.[38]

We are living through a certain crisis in relationships today; a certain disconnect between words and practice, between what we say we feel and how we act based on that feeling. This cowardice in discourse is precisely the incoherence that can be seen as a mark of our time. It is possible to say "I miss you" without ever actually making the move to set a date; it is possible to say "I like you" while practicing emotional distancing; it is possible to declare one's love while cultivating a rigid defense of one's own narcissism.

---

37 Ferraz, 2015, p. 75.

38 Foucault, 2011.

*Loving someone is not just **feeling:** it is that too, but it is also a daily **practice** of choice, which implies honesty and coherence.*

Being affectively responsible for what we offer means being able to recognize that words and silences have consequences in the other person's life, and that both our presence and our absence can shape expectations, affections, and pain.

The courage that love requires is not great, it is simply extraordinary. It takes courage not to control, not to manipulate, not to disappear, not to use the other as a mirror or source of pleasure! It is truly necessary to undress oneself and sustain the fragility of our own humanity before the fragility of another.

POSSIBLE LOVE

Is when we understand and recognize that every action, including not acting, has an impact on the other.

The courage-vulnerability axis is the heart and, perhaps, at the same time, the main failure of modern love, because, in order to be vulnerable, one has to be brave; and, in order to be brave, one has to acknowledge vulnerability with enough emotional resources to sustain it, which inevitably brings us to the time factor.

Affective responsibility, or what we might call emotional accountability, cannot be measured only by what we say today, but above all by what we are able to sustain tomorrow. Possible love demands time and calls us to look carefully at affection, not only as an event, but as a construction.

Chapter 14

The fear system

"We must build dikes of courage
to hold back the flood of fear."
– **Martin Luther King Jr.,** ***Strength to Love***

In Romeo and Julia's story, when everything finally seemed to fit together and flow, after months of dating, exchanges, and concrete actions, something in Romeo began to retract; the same man who had seemed so determined and constant became distant, confused, and cold. In Julia and Phil's story, fear reappears and is, in fact, even named by him before he disappears completely: "I think I am afraid to find out if things will work out or not." Fear seems to have been the main character, or perhaps the villain, in the story of Julia's relationships; but this does not happen only to her. In almost all modern love stories, it seems we go through the same script over and over again: intensity, desire, passion, fear, flight.

Why do we sabotage love before it even has the chance to flourish? Why does fear appear precisely when the connection deepens and intimacy begins to take form?

Maybe fear is the true test of love; the moment when idealization gives way to the real. It is when the body remembers past losses and activates old defenses, confusing protection with distance. Neuroscience and attachment theory help us understand this turning point: the moment when the body, previously driven by the desire for dopamine and by the fantasy of fusion, activates older defense systems: fear, flight, control. We will go deeper into this territory, where biology and emotion intertwine, so that we can understand how the panic of separation, the fear of dependency, and the desire for safety can coexist within us, sabotaging the very experience of loving. Understanding this paradox may be the first step toward possible love.

The Estonian-American neuroscientist Jaak Panksepp (1943-2017) stood out for investigating fundamental emotions in mammals, seeking to understand their origin and the way they relate to psychological disorders in humans.[39] For him, emotions are based in the subcortical areas of the brain, especially in the limbic system, ancient structures from an evolutionary point of view, shared by all mammals.

These areas are responsible not only for physiological and behavioral reactions, but also for the subjective and affective experience of emotions. After completing a series of postdoctoral fellowships in England and in the United States, Jaak Panksepp became a professor at Bowling Green State University in Ohio, directing his research toward the neurobiological mechanisms of attachment and social bonds. With his team, he mapped brain circuits and identified the neurochemical basis associated with "separation distress",

39 Panksepp, 1998.

an emotion he later named the PANIC/GRIEF system. His studies on social attachment were probably influenced by the discoveries made in the 1970s regarding cerebral opioid receptors, which came before his deeper contact with attachment theory, as formulated by John Bowlby.[40]

In his studies, Panksepp described seven primary affective systems:[41]

- SEEKING (Search/Expectancy)
- RAGE (Anger)
- FEAR (Anxiety)
- LUST (Sexual desire)
- CARE (Nurturance)
- PANIC/GRIEF (Separation distress)
- PLAY (Social joy)

Here, we will explore the FEAR and PANIC/GRIEF systems, which are fundamental to understanding defense and attachment responses in human beings. Both circuits are programmed to promote survival. But they operate in distinct ways and activate different behaviors in the face of danger and loss.

The FEAR system

The fear system (FEAR) is associated with detecting and responding to external threats. It is the system that activates defensive behaviors such as fight, flight, or

40 Panksepp & Biven, 2012.

41 Panksepp, 1998.

freezing, in the face of a predator or environmental danger. This system is mediated mainly by structures such as the amygdala, the hypothalamus, and the midbrain (the periaqueductal gray region), and prepares the organism to avoid physical destruction.

In human beings, beyond physical dangers, FEAR can be triggered by symbolic threats, such as rejection, judgment, or emotional exposure, especially in people with a history of insecure bonds.

The PANIC/GRIEF system

The PANIC/GRIEF system is the circuit of separation protest and social grief. It evolved to ensure that offspring, and social individuals, maintain proximity to their attachment figures. When separation or loss occurs, this system is activated, generating behaviors of searching, crying, and emotional pain, in an attempt to restore the lost bond.

The brain areas involved include the anterior cingulate cortex, the septum, and the endogenous opioid system, which modulate the pain of absence. This is the system that explains, for example, the anguish of abandonment and rejection, the desire to seek the other when they disappear from sight, as in ghosting, and the psychic pain of loneliness.

The difference between FEAR and PANIC/GRIEF

FEAR reacts to danger in the environment; its focus is to avoid physical harm.

PANIC/GRIEF reacts to the loss of the bond; its focus is to restore social connection.

Although both can be activated in contexts of threat to well-being, FEAR moves us away from what threatens us, while PANIC drives us to seek the other. In the context of attachment, this explains why some people run away from love as if it were a predator (FEAR), while others cling to the other as the only source of emotional survival (PANIC/GRIEF).

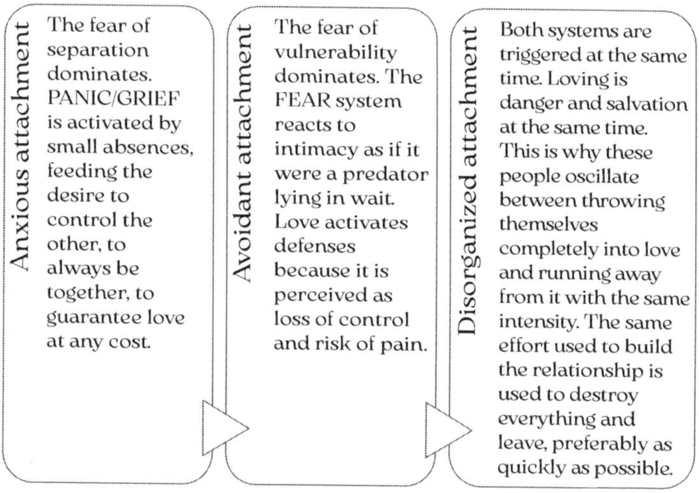

In the context of love, the danger is not a predator lying in wait. But the fear system does not distinguish between a lion in the savanna and the possibility of rejection, abandonment, or humiliation. For those who carry insecure bonds in their life story, with caregivers who were sources of pain, unpredictability, or neglect, love activates the alarm. The desire to connect coexists with the feeling of threat. And this is where the strategies of insecure attachment become established: anxious, avoidant, or disorganized.

How do we select which experiences are safe and which may be threatening?

We may already have read or heard somewhere about how our brains are innately prepared to detect situations of threat, danger, and safety, and how this system is an essential part of the survival of any species. Through our sensory organs, we detect new situations and quickly inform our system about what is happening.

For example: when we see, hear, touch, taste, or smell something, a series of new pieces of information are generated and many others are retrieved through the memories we have created about certain experiences. Then chemical and electrical signals are sent to our central and peripheral nervous systems, informing our body about this new stimulus and directing us toward decision-making, in order to preserve our integrity and safety as much as possible. This is, basically, the system of neuroception: an automatic, unconscious system for detecting danger, threat, or safety. According to the neuroscientist Stephen Porges, researcher and creator of polyvagal theory, "Neuroception explains why a baby coos at a caregiver but cries at a stranger, or why a toddler enjoys a parent's embrace but views a hug from a stranger as an assault."[42] The child has probably already formed memories that, with the parents, the environment is safe, while with a stranger, it may not be.

---

42 Porges, 2011.

Therefore, the child begins to distinguish moments of protection from moments of threat and, from that, certain reactions become possible.

The possible reactions to a stressful situation are not entirely unfamiliar to any of us: fight, flight, and freeze are the most popular, but there is also a fourth possibility, known as "fawn"[43], or the appeasing response. It is the quick reaction of trying to please the other in order to avoid conflict, often developed from childhood trauma, especially when the abuse came from an aggressor, usually an authoritarian adult, whether the abuse was verbal, moral, physical, or sexual.

Stephen Porges's polyvagal theory deepens our understanding of how the autonomic nervous system participates in states of safety, threat, and connection, showing that the autonomic nervous system does not only react to danger, but also orchestrates our way of being with the other.

> *When we feel safe, our parasympathetic nervous system, especially the ventral branch of the vagus nerve, allows us to relax, connect, listen, touch, look into someone's eyes. It is the state in which love can be born. It is that feeling we have with someone who makes us feel "at home".*

But when fear takes control, the body leaves this "connection mode" and enters a defensive state: fight, flight, freeze, or fawn. The heart accelerates, the muscles tense, the senses close down, and listening becomes selective

43 Walker, 2013.

toward whatever threatens. The other stops being a partner and becomes a potential enemy. And love becomes almost impossible, because the nervous system has already armed itself to survive, not to surrender.

When we interweave the theories, we can see how these systems connect, activate, and deactivate:

Secure attachment
The PANIC/GRIEF system is quickly deactivated because the caregiver responds to the baby's protest. The FEAR system is mobilized only in real situations of danger, and when activated, it can be better regulated.

Anxious attachment
The PANIC/GRIEF system remains chronically activated: the protest is long because the caregiver responds unpredictably.

Avoidant attachment
The PANIC/GRIEF system is suppressed and FEAR dominates: seeking the other brings more danger than comfort, so the baby, and later the adult, inhibits the protest and emotionally disconnects to avoid pain.

Disorganized attachment
The attachment system and the fear system come into conflict: the caregiver is simultaneously a source of safety and threat. The FEAR system and the PANIC/GRIEF system are activated in a confusing and contradictory way, causing the well-known behaviors of push and pull, approach and withdrawal.

If fear and the desire for control move us away from love, the way out is not to eliminate fear. That would be absolutely impossible and even undesirable; fear is vital to our survival. The path toward possible love may be to learn to recognize fear, understand it, and create new responses to it, which necessarily involves a process of self-knowledge, persistence, and relational investment. We are not born knowing how to love, much less how to love someone so different from ourselves. That is why love requires practice, learning, adjustments in direction, time, and effort.

> **POSSIBLE LOVE**
>
> The path for a possible love may be learning how to recognize fear, understand it and create new ways of responding to it.

If we love someone but do not know what to do with that love, the first step may be to open space for something different to happen.

- When you begin to fall in love with someone, what is your first reaction?
- What are your strategies when the fear of getting attached appears?
- Do you try to come closer, run away, oscillate?

Understanding and naming our reactions in the face of feelings can help us increase our perception of when we are acting on autopilot.

Loving involves a certain degree of discomfort: the discomfort of surrender, risk, and uncertainty. Especially when a relationship is still at the beginning. The solution, if there is one, does not seem to lie in avoiding this discomfort, but in staying with it. When you feel fear arising, the impulse to run away, to cling, to dissociate: stop, breathe, feel.

It is in this space between fear and automatic action that something new can be born. As Guimarães Rosa wrote: "What life wants from us is courage."[44]

And love does too.

44 The Brazilian writer João Guimarães Rosa, in his 1956 novel Grande Sertão: Veredas.

Chapter 15

Time and affection

"We drown in a glass of water because, in general, we are the size of it; we think small in time."
– **Lúcia Helena Galvão**

Time is not only a chronological measure, time is, among many things, the substance of affection and, consequently, affection has the power to change our perception of time.

The Lebanese poet Kahlil Gibran writes, in his book *The Prophet*, that we think small when it comes to time, because our perception revolves around days, months, maybe a couple of years. However, there is the clock time and there is the soul time. He distinguishes, in a poetic way, chronological time from the time of affection, a time that does not follow the rules of metrics.

When we have a joyful moment, a moment of happiness, we do not want it to end; when we are happy, we experience a time that seems to go very fast, and, quite often, when we feel sad or bored, we experience time in such a way that it seems it is never going to end. We create a narrative for time through affections, introducing nostalgia, love or anger in a past memory; we increase or decrease the emotional load of an instant; we have this extreme need of giving meaning to what was lived. Affection and time are intimately connected.

The modern subject seems to suffer from a "loss of the narrative of time" especially of a time that can be lived with meaning and continuity. This crisis is not only external: it disorganizes internally our individual experience and creates exhaustion, apathy and anguish.

We experience a kind of time that passes in a different way, not because time has changed—the measure of time continues to be the same (60 minutes are still one hour). But we change the way we interact with time. The South Korean philosopher Byung-Chul Han captures this brilliantly in his critique of the society of performance and acceleration. In *The Scent of Time*[45], he says that we have lost the capacity to experience duration. This has to do not only with the acceleration of time, but also with a certain desynchrony, a fragmentation of linear time into disconnected instants: fragmented attention, excess information, infinite stimuli… As if we were living in an eternal updating of our feeds, an eternal loop of random notifications that drag us away from the present moment and stop us from having more meaningful and lasting experiences. The quality of time is affected and, with it, our capacity to contemplate. Han says that the multiplication of events, information and images makes giving things their time impossible. The incapacity to linger is, for him, the central theme of the modern temporality crisis; modern time is accelerated, empty and

45 Han, 2017.

directionless [...] We live in a constant impossibility of concluding and remaining. "Instead of leisurely strolling around, people run from one event to another, from one piece of information to another, and from one image to another" ... And, of course, from one person to another.[46]

According to Han, the atomization of life is also an "atomization of identity": each person becomes only their "little ego", thus losing the capacity for "being-with".

Mitsein (being-with), a central concept in Martin Heidegger's philosophy, refers to the fundamental condition of the human being (*Dasein*) of always already being inserted in and related to other beings in the world; it is not only about being physically together, but rather, an ontological structure of existence: the human being is, from the beginning, a being-with-others.[47]

The disappearance of the other is a pathological symptom of the present, according to Han. The limitless connection provided by digital media weakens bonds; the person turns more and more toward themselves. The scarcity of real interactions can seriously harm empathic abilities and emotional regulation, making affective relationships difficult, especially lasting ones, which have empathy, vulnerability, and availability for the other as their basic premises.

What we see is an increase in casual and ephemeral relationships, whether friendships or romantic ones.

---

46 Han, 2017.

47 Heidegger, [1927] 2010, §§ 25–27.

These relationships happen quickly, but end even more quickly. Recreational relationships, although pleasurable and even necessary at several moments in life, do not replace the need to establish mutual trust and secure bonds. Ultimately, the act of creating bonds can evoke, in the subject who has not learned how to do so, a feeling of insecurity and threat in the face of losing oneself, besides an emotional dysregulation that leads them to avoid any kind of relationship or secure bond.

The same logic that fragments time also fragments our relationships, our bonds, and even the way we feel. In Han's terms, this atomization of affection might be the great mark of our contemporary world: a sequence of emotional impulses, intermittent stimuli, dispersed contacts that do not organize themselves into a story.

This logic of emotional discontinuity creates a kind of affective paresthesia: a certain anesthesia of deep feelings. The heart stumbles, just as time does, to borrow Han's image. There is no longer a compass, and affection, which can only develop with time and trust, has no space to mature. Without the capacity for duration, without contemplation, love is replaced by impatient excitement, by a game of seduction. We are addicted to seduction, but have little capacity to sustain what comes next; we have lost the capacity to linger. In an impatient relationship, one without narrative, connection loses its internal coherence; it becomes liking without sustaining, desiring without remaining. The atomization of affection creates a new form of affective experience that does not organize itself in time.

Contemplation is the time and space we give to something so it can flourish, without knowing exactly what comes next. Han says that the acceleration and atomization of time prevent us from sustaining long and complex processes, such as a relationship. We tend to interpret complexity and tension as structural failure, rather than as a natural part of the affective process. This leads to quick breakups, premature giving up, and unresolved patterns of closeness and avoidance.

As he says, society is dominated by the verb "can", where everything is initiative and project; therefore, we cannot enter love, with its innate quality of wounding and passion. The encounter with the other only manifests itself through the "not-being-able-to-be-able", as Han says.[48] If it were possible to possess, to grasp, and to know the other, they would no longer be the other; there is an irreducible alterity to which we do not have access and which we cannot dominate. We can only establish a lasting loving relationship if we give up, or at least regulate, our need for dominance, for power over the other.

In the dynamics of dominance, we transform love into a project, measuring who is bigger and who is smaller, watching all the time to know where we can win or lose. More than a game in which whoever cares less wins, love also becomes a game of dominance, in

48 Han, [2012] 2017.

which we cannot give more affection than we receive. We enter a subverted logic according to which being smaller does not mean being cared for by the other in a functional domination, but rather being submitted to the other; therefore, being dominated in the sense of losing the game... We are living love as if it were a big casino and we were sitting at a big poker table, always alert and trying to find the smallest signs that could show when and how we might experience a loss (so we can shield ourselves, because losing is no longer on the table...)

On the other hand, this dispersion of affection and this game of dominance create affective exhaustion and a feeling of relational defeat. Many people report having given up trying: they go out with others in order to feel something, but cannot truly connect. There may be a meeting of bodies and, quite often, good conversation, but no real connection or continuity. This brings a lot of helplessness and a certain turning off of interest in the other; a turning off of curiosity, of searching, and, in particular, of playing.

Here, I want to highlight playing, because the complexity of loving the other has roots in the complex simplicity of the capacity to play. This is because playing goes beyond thought, feeling and the inner and outer world; playing is an encounter, an encounter of internal and external possibilities, of the self and the other; playing with myself and playing with the other happen in different and simultaneous ways. Playing is in the middle, it is what moves between fantasy and reality, it has a certain poetic license to exist and a certain freedom.

The magic of playing is a universal phenomenon, just like love. Both have similar characteristics that involve our creativity, imagination, curiosity, action, illusion, excitement, disappointment, failure, reconstruction, fun, responsibility, among many other capacities that we build throughout our childhood and even in our adult life as well.

Playing is doing, it is action! When we play, something is built, and that building is necessarily relational. Free play is spontaneous, creative, improvised and does not follow strict rules. This is precisely why playing is the place where the child learns about themselves, about the other, about boundaries, about affection, about frustration, about time, about lingering and waiting. Let's think about it...

- What happens when we lose our ability to play?
- Is it possible to say that, due to the digitalization of playing, we can lose (or drastically decrease) our capacity to love?
- As individuals, are we immersed in a hopeless and passive society, losing the capacity to bet, to take risks, and to enter a world of illusions that once placed us in relation to others?

The neuroscientist Jaak Panksepp brings, as one of the central points of his work, the idea that play is not merely fun, but a neurological mechanism for regulating hierarchies, modulating dominance, and producing cooperation. He identified and mapped primary emotional systems in mammalian brains and discovered, through his research, that when rats played with one another, they produced specific sounds. When this play was reproduced with the researchers themselves, the rats continued to produce the same sounds, a certain joyful laughter, making the researchers even more curious about an ability common to all mammals: the ability to play.

Panksepp and his team were the first to develop standardized techniques to study play in the laboratory and, so far, they have discovered that there is at least one system that controls physical and social play: the PLAY system. As he writes, "It is now certain that a genetically determined PLAY network that mediates positive affect exists in mammalian brains."[49] This system is responsible for generating playful behaviors and is fundamental to the creation of social bonds, as well as to the development of emotional and cognitive abilities. Moreover, play can also be an essential tool in the construction of many of the higher functions of our social brains, "helping young animals learn to identify the individuals with whom they can develop cooperative relationships and to know whom they should avoid."

One of the most meaningful discoveries of that research was the role play has in brain development. Panksepp

49 Panksepp & Biven, 2012, p. 352.

showed that social playing activates specific areas of the brain that are essential for emotional regulation and social learning. By engaging in play, we not only have fun, but also strengthen the neural circuits associated with empathy, cooperation, and conflict resolution, crucial skills for life in society, and for love.

By playing, the individual experiences the alternation between dominating and being dominated, between winning and losing; there must be, however, a balance, since rigid, continuous, and one-sided dominance demotivates playing. In his studies, Panksepp observed that playing stops immediately when one of the individuals insists on maintaining absolute control or repeatedly imposing themselves through force. This pattern shows that dominance is only tolerable when it is flexible; otherwise, it triggers the neural systems of threat, interrupting the circuit of playful pleasure.

Playing, therefore, works as a social and emotional regulator. It is the way through which we learn to modulate dominance. This means that the quality of the bond is directly connected to the capacity of playing, when we can sustain alterity and keep the plasticity of roles.

> *A relationship in which one cannot play is a relationship in which one cannot make their own power structure flexible, a relationship that gradually loses the capacity to maintain cooperation and affective vitality.*

Playing presupposes trusting the other, a field of co-creation where a mistake is not the end, but the beginning. Jessica Benjamin writes beautifully about this, showing that, from the very beginning, playful interactions between mother and baby are not only a way to pass time, but acts of recognition.[50] And this co-creation is the basis of a healthy relationship, because it is about sustaining alterity.

- I see you.
- I validate what you feel.
- I follow you in the game.

This dynamic does not end in childhood, but is constantly reinvented in adult relationships, whether they are friendships, work relationships or loving ones.

Children rehearse this all the time: one takes the toy from the other and dominates, the other cries, the first one gives it back, the two go back to playing. The playing was interrupted, but the bond can be reestablished.

POSSIBLE LOVE

Playing teaches us to love, time teaches us that affection develops in continuity, in the possibility of rupture/reparation and in the alternation. It is in repetition and in restarting the game that the bond strengthens itself.

50 Benjamin, 1988.

The way we play, or do not play, with the other says a lot about our capacity to enter an intermediary field of love, in which meaning is created between two people. It also says a lot about our capacity, or incapacity, to tolerate ruptures and seek repair. And it strengthens us, so we can stay and begin again.

Chapter 16

To bloom and begin again

"This time it was more down-to-earth and less romantic: the love of someone who had already suffered for love."

– **Clarice Lispector**

We talk so much about love, all the songs, poems, and all the bar stories told by friends, everything revolves around relationships and love. We talk all the time, but perhaps we do not really know what it is; perhaps we know even less about how to receive love. It seems obvious, but it is not; not everyone has been loved and not everyone has been loved by that certain someone, in that certain way.

The most common thing is to seek love and push it away, that is, beginning the sabotaging process when someone reciprocates, when they return our affection, care, and desire. We begin to imagine that this person cannot possibly love us like that—that they must be needy or have ulterior motives, somehow. It seems so much easier to love someone when we are not reciprocated, and this is directly connected to our ability, or lack thereof, to know how to receive love, to allow ourselves to be loved. This is why, many times, we try to get closer to someone who confirms that we do not deserve to be loved; we unconsciously seek relationships that place us in a position we have been in before, and that produce a kind of suffering that is already known, uncomfortable, but familiar.

These dysfunctional relationships, such as loving someone who does not love us back, seem like madness... Who would consciously choose that? Yet we do choose them, in a kind of warped way, based on childhood stories and even on previous relationships that did not work out. The story we tell ourselves is that we are unlovable, that we are not worthy of true love, that no one stays, that they only want to use us... Our creativity is endless when it comes to this.

Moreover, when you learn to be too independent, to solve everything, to make decisions alone, to take care of your own life, you quite often begin to lose the ability to let go, to trust, and to receive, whether it is a small gesture of care, a kind gesture that makes you feel guilty or distrustful, or someone paying a bill, making dinner for you, planning a date, giving you a massage, giving you a gift, caring about your well-being, taking care of you.

Our traumas make us so independent, self-sufficient, self-sabotaging, and protected inside our own little dragon cave that, when we receive something, we do not quite know how to respond to it:

- Thank them?
- Retribute?
- Feel guilty?
- Feel scared?
- Run away?

When we receive love and have not yet developed the capacity to receive it freely, without seeing it as something strange, as a possible threat, we begin the process of eliminating that threat. It is as if we had installed a "psychological antivirus", the same kind as the ones we install on computers: any sign of depth and real emotional proximity is treated as a threat.

It is as if the system were already there, running. Then, we meet someone who offers something more and awakens something more in us. This person gets past the initial safety barriers and the system triggers the alert: "Danger, danger! We have a security breach." A silent notification pops up: "Vulnerability detected." And it was love, the possibility of being seen: real and reciprocated affection.

After that, the system, very well programmed, begins to eliminate the risk: it creates distance, cuts off the connection, sends delayed messages, closes windows, and puts up barriers. If necessary, it shuts down the whole system, to stop the intruder from accessing too much. We initiate the fight, flight, or freeze process; our emotions become dysregulated and, the more avoidant and scared we are, the more we shut down the system, cutting off communication and pushing the other away from our lives. We begin to test the relationship, doing the most twisted things, just to see if the other stays or leaves, in the hope that they will stay and love us, but also secretly rooting for them to go and confirm our failure. As Freud wrote: "It is that we are never so defenseless against suffering as when we love, never so helplessly unhappy as when we have lost our loved object or its love".[51]

Possible love only happens when we manage to overcome that barrier. We have to let go, we need to develop trust in the other and in our own "lovability", our own capacity to be loved by someone, just as we are. We need to trust the other more and our destructive narratives less.

The practice of secure love demands trust, hope, and a healthy dose of recognition of the whole process that is taking place, a certain helplessness, so that we can then fight against what happens inside us. In other words, receiving love implies bearing the helplessness that affection stirs in us.

Do you remember Julia?

Julia was always drawn to confusing emotions. Her history of chaotic relationships dated back to well before Romeo; her family patterns were not exactly trustworthy. Stories of rejection, abandonment, and an endless attempt to fix the other permeated the narrative of Julia's relationships and, of course, of her masculine models.

After a first dramatic teenage love at fifteen, Julia closed herself off from relationships and became someone who avoided any kind of intimacy; she could not get deeply involved with anyone, had trouble believing she could be loved by someone who would stay by her side and, at the slightest sign of love, ran away. Until, after a few small

---

51 Freud, 1930, p. 82.

disasters and a painful breakup in her twenties, Julia sought professional help. Slowly, she began to understand herself and her relationship patterns.

Still hurt by the fact that she had recently ended a relationship, in a situation that was rather confusing, Julia met Vinicius at university. They both developed a mutual interest and began to get romantically involved. Julia, realizing she was in love and invested, noticed that she wanted to flee. She was afraid of everything that could happen again: being cheated on, rejected, abandoned; all her fears came together and created a pressure that led her to face them and to be brave enough to open up about them. Vini decided to ask Julia to be his girlfriend two months after they met, and Julia, not quite knowing how to put what she felt into words, told him in the only way she knew how:

— I found out I have a problem. I will do everything to push you away because this is what I do when I like someone.

— You can try; do your best, but I will still be here. — Vini replied.

That moment changed Julia's life forever. But not just that moment, all the other moments in the years that followed, because Vini's confidence was real; it was not just words or excitement, it was someone willing to build something bigger, to renounce some of his own needs so he could understand, support, and love Julia.

On the other hand, Julia made an effort and was brave enough to face her fears, to be vulnerable, and to allow herself to be loved, even while struggling with that feeling of not deserving to be loved, which was always lurking, but no longer prevailed or got in the way of the relationship.

Sometimes, in order to begin again, we have to finish some unfinished business, both internally and externally. Maybe this is why myths remain alive: because they speak precisely to those deeply human places where we need to make conscious choices and decide whether we keep going or remain stuck, whether in the past or in our own narratives that no longer fit us. One of these myths is the myth of Orpheus and Eurydice.

As Greek mythology tells us, Orpheus was the son of the muse Calliope and the god Apollo, and when he played his lyre, which, depending on the origin of the myth, he either invented or received as a gift from Apollo, miraculous things happened: stones moved, wild animals were soothed, and river waters became completely still. He loved the nymph Eurydice, who, in the most famous version of the story, died after being bitten by a snake, while trying to escape Aristaeus, a beekeeper who pursued her.[52]

Orpheus, heartbroken by the death of his beloved, furious at what had happened, and completely taken over by profound sadness, asked Zeus to intercede. Zeus said he could not, but that Orpheus should try to speak with his brother, Hades, the god of the underworld. The young musician took his lyre and went down into Hades' domain, using music to convince Charon, the ferryman, to let him through, and making Cerberus, the monstrous three-headed dog, fall asleep with a beautiful melody.

---

52 Virgil, Georgics IV; Ovid, Metamorphoses X.

When he stood before Hades and Persephone, lords of the realm of the dead, Orpheus played and sang the pain of losing Eurydice. Even the gods were moved by the music. Hades, who rarely made exceptions, agreed to allow Eurydice to return to the world of the living, with only one condition: Orpheus had to walk in front of her, guiding her out of the underworld, without looking back, until both were under the sunlight. If he looked back before they were out, Eurydice would be lost forever.

They were together again! It only seemed like a simple demand, but it was a long, silent, and dark crossing. Orpheus could hear the light footsteps behind him, or maybe it was just the echo. He was not sure she was following him, he could not confirm her presence, he needed to trust and keep walking through the darkness, even without being sure that his beloved would survive.

When he finally saw the first streak of light marking the exit from the Realm of the Dead, anguish won. At the threshold, only a few steps from the surface, overtaken by the fear of being tricked or of having lost his beloved once again, Orpheus turned his face and looked back.

At that moment, Eurydice fell to the ground, lifeless, and was dragged back to the underworld. Orpheus tried to return, but this time, the gates were closed.

- How many times do we let what could have been escape, just because we needed proof that only time could provide?
- How can we trust what we cannot control?

- What do we need to leave behind so we can begin again?

As Clarice wrote: love does not end. It is as if the world were waiting for me. And I go toward what waits for me.

And you?

Possible love requires a hovering flight

"When you reach the end of what you should know,
you will be at the beginning of what you should sense."
– **Khalil Gibran, Sand and Foam**

This quote from Gibran feels like the perfect opening for the end, and the end for a new beginning. The transition from **modern love to possible love** may happen when we begin to recognize the limits of the intellect in the face of human experience. It is time for us to stop thinking so much, stop rationalizing everything, and allow ourselves to feel. That is when we give up controlling the other, controlling time and affection, and begin to accept what we have, what we chose, what we are living, without being so afraid, so worried, and with much more spontaneity and, above all, courage. Just like the flight of a hummingbird, possible love requires a more stable kind of flight, a certain lingering.

In the end, it seems to me that love is what does not fit into any theory; especially in this time when we need, or desire, to decipher everything before living it. Love has been suffering its decline, the crisis is real, but, even so, it is resistance, because it remains in the field of not-knowing, of the untamable. We can try to avoid it; however, sooner or later, it finds us.

To love is, without a doubt, a choice. But not just the affective choice of being with someone; it is the choice to allow ourselves to be transformed, the choice to let love come and break who we were in order to build a new self from what is left. Love is a mirror, not in the narcissistic sense, but in the sense that the other shows us who we are. And, if we do not like who we are, we will either break the mirror or transform ourselves, to be willing to cross the emotional river and learn to swim in our emotions without drowning… until we get to the other side!

No one comes unscathed from a love story, nor from a passion, and even less from an almost-love.

In our avoidant world, we have created an entire system based on fear and emotional withdrawal, shaping the way we love. And this is not a metaphor; it is the description of a time in which intimacy has become too risky and the difficulty of making choices leads us into an emotional labyrinth. We urgently need to find a way out.

On one of my many walks throughout the world, I met a traveling woman in her seventies who told me she had lived an intense love story when she was young and that, after thirty years, she met this old love again. She told me he had always been the one who moved her the most, but, because of the relationship struggles they had back then, they had to separate; and, when they met again, it seemed the feeling was still alive, very much as it had been so many years before. They both decided to restart their relationship and finally live their love. But, after a while, she understood that he could not give her what she needed in this life, and they decided to go their separate ways. Even so, she told me she loved him, she had never stopped.

We may love, and still be unable to adjust our emotional and physical needs in order to be with someone; this does not mean that love has ended. On the contrary, maybe true love is the one that endures mismatched encounters, the one that goes through the end of the relationship and still remains with us. Even when we know we cannot have the other as our romantic partner in this life, love remains alive in our memories and present in many other ways.

Possible love is not so much an overwhelming romance as it is a choice, like the hovering flight of the hummingbird, which can flap its wings up to eighty times per second. That is much more work than simply flying away with the help of the wind. It looks simple, but it is just like possible love: it demands an internal effort and a kind of work that may seem invisible, but builds unimaginable bridges within us, and outside us as well.

Many years ago, I wrote a poem that goes:

I could explain it through theories
Describe it with phenomenology
Name it through a thousand psychologies
What I cannot reach in analysis
What poets try to hold in sentences
What music builds in melodies
What composers turn into harmonies
But this, what I feel, is everything that escapes me.

May we escape this avoidant logic, may we allow ourselves to affect and be affected by the other. May we love, with surrender, in times of flight. May we live possible love in an avoidant world.

THE END...
OR IS IT?

References

Ainsworth, Mary D. S., Mary C. Blehar, Everett Waters, and Sally Wall. *Patterns of Attachment: A Psychological Study of the Strange Situation.* Hillsdale, NJ: Erlbaum, 1978.

Aristotle. *Politics.* Translated by C. D. C. Reeve. Indianapolis: Hackett Publishing Company, 1998.

Augustine. *Confessions.* Translated by Henry Chadwick. Oxford: Oxford University Press, 1991.

Augustine. *On Free Choice of the Will.* Translated by Thomas Williams. Indianapolis: Hackett Publishing Company, 1993.

Benjamin, Jessica. *Beyond Doer and Done To: Recognition Theory, Intersubjectivity and the Third.* London: Routledge, 2018.

Benjamin, Jessica. *Like Subjects, Love Objects: Essays on Recognition and Sexual Difference.* New Haven: Yale University Press, 1995.

Benjamin, Jessica. *Shadow of the Other: Intersubjectivity and Gender in Psychoanalysis.* New York: Routledge, 1997.

Benjamin, Jessica. *The Bonds of Love: Psychoanalysis, Feminism, and the Problem of Domination.* New York: Pantheon Books, 1988.

Birman, Joel. *Amar a si mesmo e amar o outro: narcisismo e sexualidade na psicanálise contemporânea.* Rio de Janeiro: Civilização Brasileira, 2016.

Bowlby, John. *A Secure Base: Parent-Child Attachment and Healthy Human Development.* New York: Basic Books, 1988.

Bowlby, John. *Attachment and Loss. Vol. 1, Attachment.* 2nd ed. New York: Basic Books, 1982.

Breton, André. *Mad Love.* Translated by Mary Ann Caws. Lincoln: University of Nebraska Press, 1987.

Carter, C. Sue. "Oxytocin Pathways and the Evolution of Human Behavior." *Annual Review of Psychology* 65 (2014): 17–39. https://doi.org/10.1146/annurev-psych-010213-115110.

Cintra, Elisa. "Dominar, submeter-se, libertar-se: Jessica Benjamin e os laços de amor." *Psicologia em Revista* 24, no. 3 (2018): 686–704. https://doi.org/10.5752/P.1678-9563.2018v24n3p686-704.

Couto, Mia. *O Universo num Grão de Areia*. Lisbon: Editorial Caminho, 2019.

De Martino, Ernesto. *The End of the World: Cultural Apocalypse and Transcendence*. Translated by Dorothy Louise Zinn. Chicago: University of Chicago Press, 2023.

De Vynck, Gerrit, and Jeremy B. Merrill. "We Analyzed 47,000 ChatGPT Conversations. Here's What People Really Use It For." *The Washington Post*, November 12, 2025. https://www.washingtonpost.com/technology/2025/11/12/how-people-use-chatgpt-data/.

Emanuele, E., et al. "Association between Platelet Serotonin Levels and Romantic Love." *Psychiatry Research* 149 (2007): 231–235.

Ferraz, Maria Cristina Franco. "Foucault, 1984: a coragem de *A Coragem da Verdade*." *Revista Trágica* 18, no. 2: 70–79. https://doi.org/10.59488/tragica.v18i2.68321.

Fingermann, Dominique. "Amar adentro." *Stylus* 30 (2015): 103–110.

Foucault, Michel. *The Courage of Truth: The Government of Self and Others II. Lectures at the Collège de France, 1983–1984*. Edited by Frédéric Gros. Translated by Graham Burchell. Basingstoke: Palgrave Macmillan, 2011.

Freud, Sigmund. "A Difficulty in the Path of Psycho-Analysis." In *The Standard Edition of the Complete Psychological Works of Sigmund Freud*, vol. 17, edited and translated by James Strachey, 135–144. London: Hogarth Press, 1955. First published 1917.

Freud, Sigmund. *Civilization and Its Discontents*. Translated by James Strachey. In *The Standard Edition of the Complete Psychological Works of Sigmund Freud*, vol. 21. London: Hogarth Press, 1961. First published 1930.

Freud, Sigmund. "Instincts and Their Vicissitudes." In *The Standard Edition of the Complete Psychological Works of Sigmund Freud*, vol. 14, edited and translated by James Strachey, 109–140. London: Hogarth Press, 1957.

Freud, Sigmund. "On Narcissism: An Introduction." In *The Standard Edition of the Complete Psychological Works of Sigmund Freud*, vol. 14, edited and translated by James Strachey, 67–102. London: Hogarth Press, 1957. First published 1914.

Freud, Sigmund. "Repression." In *The Standard Edition of the Complete Psychological Works of Sigmund Freud*, vol. 14, edited and translated by James Strachey, 141–158. London: Hogarth Press, 1957.

Freud, Sigmund. "The Unconscious." In *The Standard Edition of the Complete Psychological Works of Sigmund Freud*, vol. 14, edited and translated by James Strachey, 159–215. London: Hogarth Press, 1957.

Galvão, Lúcia Helena. "O Tempo, Segundo Gibran — Série O Profeta." YouTube video. Nova Acrópole Brasil. Accessed May 22, 2025. https://www.youtube.com/watch?v=si1UY48X0v4&t=1430s.

García Márquez, Gabriel. *Love in the Time of Cholera*. Translated by Edith Grossman. New York: Alfred A. Knopf, 1988.

Ghosts of Girlfriends Past. Directed by Mark Waters. Written by Jon Lucas and Scott Moore. Performances by Matthew McConaughey and Jennifer Garner. New Line Cinema, 2009. Film.

Gibran, Kahlil. *Sand and Foam: A Book of Aphorisms*. New York: Alfred A. Knopf, 1926.

Gibran, Kahlil. *The Prophet*. New York: Alfred A. Knopf, 1923.

Han, Byung-Chul. *Speaking About God: A Dialogue with Simone Weil*. Translated by Wieland Hoban. Cambridge: Polity Press, 2026.

Han, Byung-Chul. *The Agony of Eros*. Foreword by Alain Badiou. Translated by Erik Butler. Cambridge, MA: MIT Press, 2017.

Han, Byung-Chul. *The Scent of Time: A Philosophical Essay on the Art of Lingering*. Translated by Daniel Steuer. Cambridge: Polity Press, 2017.

Han, Byung-Chul. *The Tonality of Thought*. Translated by Daniel Steuer. Cambridge: Polity Press, 2024.

Hegel, G. W. F. *Phenomenology of Spirit*. Translated by A. V. Miller. Oxford: Oxford University Press, 1977.

Heidegger, Martin. *Being and Time*. Translated by Joan Stambaugh. Revised by Dennis J. Schmidt. Albany: SUNY Press, 2010. First published 1927.

Her. Directed and written by Spike Jonze. Performances by Joaquin Phoenix, Amy Adams, and Scarlett Johansson. Warner Bros. Pictures, 2013. Film.

Insel, Thomas R., and Larry E. Shapiro. "Oxytocin Receptor Distribution Reflects Social Organization in Monogamous and Polygamous Voles." *Proceedings of the National Academy of Sciences of the United States of America* 89, no. 13 (1992): 5981–5985. https://doi.org/10.1073/pnas.89.13.5981.

"Juntos." Written by Mark Ronson, Andrew Wyatt, Paula Fernandes de Souza, Stefani J. Germanotta, and Anthony Rossomando. Performed by Paula Fernandes. On *Origens*. Universal Music, 2019.

King, Martin Luther, Jr. *Strength to Love*. Philadelphia: Fortress Press, 2010. First published 1963.

Kurup, R. K., and P. A. Kurup. "Hypothalamic Digoxin, Hemispheric Dominance, and Neurobiology of Love and Affection." International Journal of Neuroscience 113, no. 5 (2003): 721–729. https://doi.org/10.1080/00207450390200107

Lacan, Jacques. *Écrits: The First Complete Edition in English*. Translated by Bruce Fink, in collaboration with Héloïse Fink and Russell Grigg. New York: W. W. Norton & Company, 2006.

Lacan, Jacques. *The Seminar of Jacques Lacan, Book VIII: Transference*. Edited by Jacques-Alain Miller. Translated by Bruce Fink. Cambridge: Polity Press, 2015.

Lady Gaga and Bradley Cooper. "Shallow." Written by Lady Gaga, Mark Ronson, Anthony Rossomando, and Andrew Wyatt. From *A Star Is Born: Original Motion Picture Soundtrack*. Interscope Records, 2018.

Langeslag, Sandra J. E. "Is the Serotonergic System Altered in Romantic Love? A Literature Review and Research Suggestions." In *Psychology of Relationships*, edited by E. Cuyler and M. Ackhart, 213–218. New York: Nova Science Publishers, 2009.

Lembke, Anna. *Dopamine Nation: Finding Balance in the Age of Indulgence*. New York: Dutton, 2021.

Lispector, Clarice. *The Hour of the Star*. Translated by Benjamin Moser. New York: New Directions, 2011.

Machado, D. de O. "A neurociência afetiva de Jaak Panksepp e suas contribuições para a compreensão dos vínculos sociais." *Revista Brasileira de Psicanálise* 52, no. 2 (2018): 45–60.

Marazziti, Donatella, Hagop S. Akiskal, Antonio Rossi, and Giovanni B. Cassano. "Alteration of the Platelet Serotonin Transporter in Romantic Love." *Psychological Medicine* 29, no. 3 (1999): 741–745.

Netflix. "Netflix Upfront 2025: The Center of Attention." *About Netflix*, May 14, 2025. https://about.netflix.com/news/netflix-upfront-2025-the-center-of-attention.

Ovid. *Metamorphoses*. Translated by Frank Justus Miller. Revised by G. P. Goold. Cambridge, MA: Harvard University Press, 1984.

Panksepp, Jaak. *Affective Neuroscience: The Foundations of Human and Animal Emotions*. New York: Oxford University Press, 1998.

Panksepp, Jaak, and Lucy Biven. *The Archaeology of Mind: Neuroevolutionary Origins of Human Emotions*. New York: W. W. Norton & Company, 2012.

Pansieri, Flávio. "Liberdade no pensamento ocidental." In *Enciclopédia Jurídica da PUC-SP*, edited by Celso Fernandes Campilongo, Alvaro de Azevedo Gonzaga, and André Luiz Freire. São Paulo: Pontifícia Universidade Católica de São Paulo, 2017. https://enciclopediajuridica.pucsp.br/verbete/114/edicao-1/liberdade-no-pensamento-ocidental,-a.

Pessoa, Fernando. *The Keeper of Sheep*. Translated by Edwin Honig and Susan M. Brown. Riverdale-on-Hudson: Sheep Meadow Press, 1986.

Porges, Stephen W. *The Polyvagal Theory: Neurophysiological Foundations of Emotions, Attachment, Communication, and Self-Regulation*. New York: W. W. Norton & Company, 2011.

Rilke, Rainer Maria. "Der Dichter." In *Neue Gedichte*. Leipzig: Insel Verlag, 1907.

Rosa, João Guimarães. *Grande Sertão: Veredas*. Rio de Janeiro: Nova Fronteira, 2001.

Sartre, Jean-Paul. *Being and Nothingness*. Translated by Hazel E. Barnes. New York: Philosophical Library, 1956.

Silva, Pablo Soares. "A parresía cínica em Diógenes de Sinope." *Controvérsia* 17, no. 1 (2021): 104–118.

Tomasevicius Filho, Eduardo. "O conceito de liberdade em Santo Agostinho." *Revista da Faculdade de Direito da Universidade de São Paulo* 101 (2006): 1079–1091.

Tronick, Ed. *The Neurobehavioral and Social-Emotional Development of Infants and Children*. New York: W. W. Norton & Company, 2007.

Virgil. *Georgics*. Translated by H. Rushton Fairclough. Revised by G. P. Goold. Cambridge, MA: Harvard University Press, 1999.

Von Franz, Marie-Louise. *Alchemy: An Introduction to the Symbolism and the Psychology*. Toronto: Inner City Books, 1980.

Walker, Pete. *Complex PTSD: From Surviving to Thriving: A Guide and Map for Recovering from Childhood Trauma*. Lafayette, CA: Azure Coyote, 2013.

Walsh, Roger, Barbara Victor, and Robin Bitner. "Emotional Effects of Sertraline: Novel Findings Revealed by Meditation." *American Journal of Orthopsychiatry* 76, no. 1 (2006): 134–137. https://doi.org/10.1037/0002-9432.76.1.134.

Westphal, Sarah. "Quase." Originally published on Sarah Westphal's blog in 2002. Available at: https://tinyurl.com/5n85znvv. Accessed May 22, 2025.

Winnicott, D. W. "Letter 26: To Roger Money-Kyrle, 27 November 1952." In *The Spontaneous Gesture: Selected Letters of D. W. Winnicott*, edited by F. Robert Rodman. Cambridge, MA: Harvard University Press, 1987.

Winnicott, D. W. "Mirror-Role of Mother and Family in Child Development." In *Playing and Reality*. London: Routledge, 2005. First published 1971.

Winnicott, D. W. *Playing and Reality*. London: Routledge, 2005. First published 1971.

Winnicott, D. W. *The Maturational Processes and the Facilitating Environment: Studies in the Theory of Emotional Development*. London: Hogarth Press, 1965.

Winnicott, D. W. "The Mother-Infant Experience of Mutuality." In *Psycho-Analytic Explorations*, edited by Clare Winnicott, Ray Shepherd, and Madeleine Davis. Cambridge, MA: Harvard University Press, 1989.

Winnicott, D. W. "The Use of an Object and Relating through Identifications." In *Playing and Reality*. London: Routledge, 2005. First published 1971.

Young, Larry, and Brian Alexander. *The Chemistry Between Us: Love, Sex, and the Science of Attraction*. New York: Current, 2012.

About the Author and Contact Information

Danielle Vieira is a psychologist and psychoanalyst. She has been practicing clinically for over ten years, researching contemporary relationships, the impasses of affection, and forms of emotional avoidance in today's world. She lives between countries, an experience that permeates both her writing and her clinical listening.

Website: www.daniellevieira.com.br

E-mail: contato@daniellevieira.com.br

Instagram: @danielle_vieira

Typography Adobe Garamond Pro, Arsenica and Butik
Paper Pólen Natural 80g/m^2
Printed by Paym

Made in the USA
Monee, IL
16 September 2026

63296743R00113